Again, for Norman

Liberian Proverb

*A little rain each day will
fill the rivers to overflowing.*

HYLA DOC IN AFRICA

1950-1961

Edited by Elsie H. Landstrom

Elsie H. Landstrom

Q.E.D. Press

Fort Bragg, California

Hyla Doc in Africa, 1950-1961
Copyright © 1994 by Elsie H. Landstrom

Published by QED Press
155 Cypress Street
Fort Bragg, California 95437

Publicist: Elizabeth S. Allen
520 Old Post Road
Tolland, Connecticut 06084

Printed in the U.S.A.

First edition

Library of Congress Cataloging in Publications Data
Hyla Doc.
  Hyla Doc in Africa, 1950-1961 / edited by Elsie H. Landstrom.
    p. cm.
  Sequel to: Hyla Doc: surgeon in China through war and revolution, 1924–1949.
ISBN 0-936609-32-X
  1. Hyla Doc. 2. Surgeons—United States—Biography
3. Surgeons—Liberia—Biography. 4. Missionaries, Medical—Liberia—Biography. 5. Mano (African people)—Medical care—History. 6. Ganta United Methodist Mission—Employees—Biography. I. Landstrom, Elsie H. II. Title.
RD27.35.H95A3 1994
966.6203'092—dc20
[B]   93-6280
                                    CIP

Cover photo, *Hyla Doc in 1987*, by Jennifer Curry
Back cover photo, *Gio mask,* gift from Hyla Doc to the Smith College Museum of Art, reproduced courtesy of the museum.

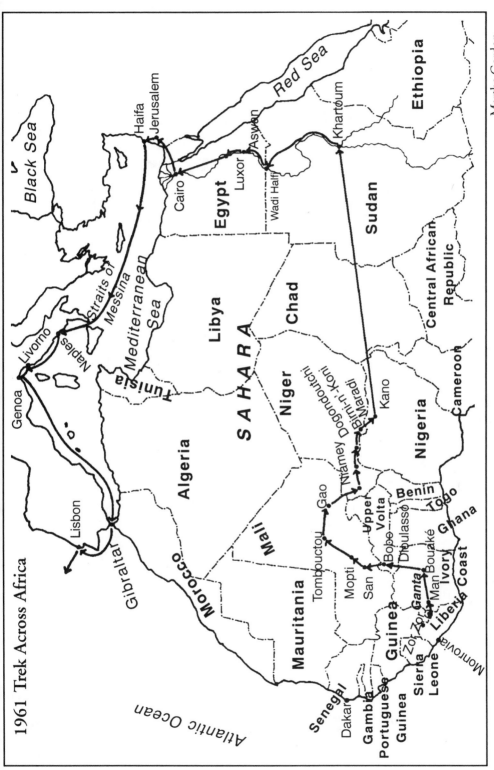

1961 Trek Across Africa

Martha Gordon

Acknowledgments

The African journal kept jointly by Hyla S. Watters and Mildred Black from which the story of their journey across Africa was shaped, and the record of Hyla Doc's work at Ganta Mission taken from letters she wrote to her family, are now in safekeeping in the Sophia Smith Collection and Smith College Archives.

My gratitude to Mary Maples Dunn, President of Smith College, who encouraged the project from its inception, raised helpful questions and made other resources of the college available to me.

To Susan Grigg, former Director of the Sophia Smith Collection and College Archives, Margery N. Sly, College Archivist, now Acting Director, and Araina Heath, Administrative Assistant, my gratitude for their encouragement and for preparing the manuscript. Without their support and a boost from Margaret Shriver and Margaret Berry, I would still be wondering what to do with the engaging chapters regretfully omitted from *Hyla Doc, Surgeon in China Through War and Revolution, 1924–1949.*

Research for both books consisted of crawling under beds at Tupper Lake and badgering family members in search of Hyla Doc's letters. The treasure excavated added up to about one thousand single-spaced elite-typed pages, many torn and disintegrating and with wide gaps during critical periods in history when Hyla Doc could not write. These gaps were filled in with the help of letters and reminiscences of colleagues, and with stories taped by Elizabeth and Dan Allen and myself. Hyla Doc died before the writing got underway.

Mildred Black has been generous with photographs and good advice. Other photographs were supplied by Charles and Blanche Britt, Martha Cofield, Wilfred Boayue and Eugene L. Harley, son of Ganta Mission founders George W. and Winifred J. Harley. Although I have finally laid hands on photographs of Hyla and Mildred, Charles Britt suggests that our difficulties to do so stemmed from the fact that Hyla Doc seldom stood still long enough to be photographed, while Mildred was usually behind the camera.

Jennifer Curry took the cover photograph, and once again Martha Gordon has drawn our map. Margaret Berry and Doris Karsell have lent their talents and support at every point, while the support of Hyla Doc's family, especially her niece, Elizabeth Allen and that of her husband Dan Allen, has been unflagging. Cynthia Frank, John Fremont, Linda Gatter, Marla Greenway and Chuck Hathaway at QED Press, are high on my appreciation list for their reliably expert transformation of manuscript into book.

Keeping abreast of the confusing civil war raging in Liberia since December 1989 has been eased through the help of Steve Tucker, Program Manager, African Governments Program, The Carter Center of Emory University in Atlanta, Georgia; Paul McDermott, Director, the Liberia Office of the African Governments Program, and John Butin, a Graduate Research Assistant in the Conflict Resolutions Center.

All facts and ideas relating to the founding and history of Liberia are found in standard works on Liberia: Sir Harry Johnston, *Liberia* (London: Hutchinson & Co., Inc., 1906); Charles Morrow Wilson, *Liberia* (New York: William Sloane Associates, Inc., 1947); Raymond Leslie Buell, *Liberia: A Century of Survival,* 1847-1947 (Philadelphia: African Handbooks, the University of Pennsylvania Press and the University Museum, 1947); Lawrence A. Marinelli, *The New Liberia, A Historical and Political Survey* (New York, London: Frederick A. Praeger, 1964). For materials on the history of Ganta Mission I am indebted to Eugene L. Harley for the loan of his mother's book: Winifred J. Harley, *A Third of a Century with George Way Harley* (Liberian Studies Association in America, Inc., Newark, Delaware, 1973); and for permission to quote from it.

All errors are my own.

Elsie H. Landstrom, Conway, Massachusetts

Contents

Ganta Mission home of Mildred and Hya Doc. All Ganta Mission buildings were built of local materials by local craftsmen taught by George Harley.

Photo by Mildred A. Black

Mildred Black, left, and Hyla Doc admiring a frangipani

Photo courtesy of Eugene L. Harley

Hyla Watters and Mildred Black

The memoir, *Hyla Doc, Surgeon in China Through War and Revolution, 1924-1949,* was published in 1990 by QED Press. It told the story of this diminutive woman's remarkable twenty-five years in China as chief surgeon at the Wuhu General Hospital. She was under appointment by the Board of Foreign Missions of the Methodist Episcopal Church.

Into her barely four-foot-eight, Hyla Doc (so-called to distinguish her from other Hylas in her family) packed an enormous energy fueled by curiosity, an open mind and concern for the well-being of others. Compassion took precedence over her own safety, comfort or convenience, her erratic heart. She was the third child of a Methodist clergyman, Philip M. Watters, who served a number of churches in New York state, then as president of Gammon Theological Seminary in Atlanta, Georgia. In the Methodist Church of that period it was the custom to move pastors every three or four years; the summer camp at Tupper Lake in New York was the only family home Hyla Doc knew. But, secure within a loving, fun-loving and intellectually-stimulating family grounded in Christian faith, it was natural to Hyla Doc to go to and fro over the earth in response to other's needs. Beyond her gifts as a healer, Hyla Doc was a born storyteller. We are fortunate to get vivid glimpses through her eyes of the people and events of her time.

Hyla Doc's years at Smith College both fed and challenged her insatiable quest for understanding her world. She took to China the skills acquired at Cornell Medical School, Bellevue, Morristown Hospital in New Jersey and the London School of Tropical Medicine and Hygiene. Hyla Doc's quarter century in China gave her the confidence as a surgeon to tackle any problem that came her way; there was no specialty surgery in China or Liberia.

China was always at war in those days of the warlords followed by Chiang Kai-shek's attempt to unify the country. War with the Japanese, huge natural disasters and civil war with the communists caused more turmoil and suffering. Hyla Doc was interned by the Japanese for nearly two years before being repatriated to the U.S. She stayed long enough to gather medical supplies, hitched a ride on a U.S. troopship to India, (always at the ready for torpedoes), and flew over the Himalayas to reach West (Free) China. There she prepared to take back Wuhu hospital from the Japanese at the end of World War Two. She had expected to stay on under the communists, but Chinese friends convinced her that their lives were at risk if they were found to be working with her.

Hyla Doc was soon en route to Ganta, Liberia. There she learned a new language, adjusted to a new culture and enlarged medical services in the bush. At Ganta Mission she shared a bungalow with Mildred Black, an exuberant colleague who had roots in the Midwest, and who also was devoted to serving others. Mildred's father, College Engineer at Albion Methodist College in Michigan, had grown up on a farm. During several summers he also worked a quarter section in Alberta, Canada. Mildred and her sister loved the farm life and riding the horses, but the rugged and isolated life was not a happy one for their mother, an artist and teacher. The family finally sold the farm and settled back in their Michigan home.

Mildred graduated from Albion in 1932 and went on to service jobs with a Kellogg Health Camp for children with eating problems, and as recreational director at the State Hospital at Kalamazoo. For three years she was a social case worker and a group leader of Camp Fire Girls. After she took the Camp Fire Girls Executive Training at New York University, she was assigned to an executive position in New Haven.

During her college years Mildred heard Mary Weathers Camphor, widow of Alexander P. Camphor, Bishop of Africa, speak about the great needs in Africa. Bishop Camphor had been president of the College of West Africa at Monrovia while also acting as United States vice-consul for Liberia before he was elected bishop. Mrs. Camphor ignited Mildred's interest in Liberia. While Mildred was in New Haven and heard Dr. George W. and Winifred J. Harley speak about Ganta Mission, she was ready to accept their invitation and accompanied them back to Liberia in 1938. There she helped out at the clinic where 400 patients were treated each day, worked with Winifred in the laboratory and taught in the elementary school.

Mildred's greatest gift to Liberia came about because she could not endure being unable to converse freely with the Mano, the principal tribe in the Ganta area. She began to keep a written record of Mano words, and on her 1950 furlough got professional linguistic training. The Manos had never had a written script; it was Mildred who taught them to write and then to read their own language; Mildred who devised a language study course for the foreigners. On her retirement in 1975, the Republic of Liberia honored her by making her Dame Grand Commander.

Required by age to retire in 1959, Hyla Doc cajoled the powers-that-be to allow her two more years at Ganta. In 1961, never one to turn her back on adventure, she teamed up with Mildred, who had a furlough due. With a map of Africa, zest and little else, Mildred and Hyla Doc turned their backs on the easy transatlantic voyage home, and "went the other way."

On her return to Tupper Lake in 1961, Hyla Doc continued to work as a physician into her eighties, when she sold her car and with the proceeds returned to China to lecture at the medical school established by the Peoples Republic of China for which her old hospital is now the teaching hospital. She met old friends there, bringing an appropriate closure to her long life. On 3 August 1987, she died at Tupper Lake. She was almost ninety-four.

Public recognition of Hyla Doc's work came in 1950 when Smith College conferred on her the honorary degree, Doctor of Science. In 1953 she was ordained at the 120th Annual Conference of the Methodist Episcopal Church of the Republic of Liberia. In 1967 the Women's Medical Society of New York named her "Woman of the Year." And in 1969 she was honored as "Woman of All The Years" by the Business and Professional Women of Tupper Lake.

1. Stone House
   (Harley home)
2. Hospital Chapel
3. Clinic
4. Men's Ward
5. Women's Ward
6. School of Nursing
7. Utility Building
   (Laundry, Kitchen, Dining Room)
8. Laboratory
9. Stone Church
10. Doctor's home
11. Britt's home
12. First School now teacher's home
13. 14. 15. 16. School boys' houses
17. Haffen House — Hyla Doc's home
18. Gym — Auditorium (built later)
19. Elementary School
20. Boys' Dining Hall
21. Cofield's home
22. Missionary home
23. Teacher's home
24. Pastor's home
25. Worker's home
26. First Clinic — Now store house
27. Garage — Machine house
28. Saw Mill, Carpenter Shop, Blacksmith Shop
29. Diesel House (for lights, etc.)
30. Nurses home
31. Literacy Center (Mab's home)
32. Worker's home
34. 35. 36. Missionary homes
33. Jr. High — Now Sr. High

Ganta Mission, circa 1950

From a sketch by Mildred Black

Ganta Mission

In 1949 I left Wuhu, in Anhwei Province of China, a mile ahead of the communist take-over of the city. At fifty-six I wasn't about to dangle my feet and mope, and was soon on my way to Ganta, Liberia. One of my first patients was an old man who had had a bad stroke. He got worse and worse day-by-day, and it was obvious he was dying.

He got to the place where he would breathe a few times and wait a while, breathe a few times and wait a little longer, then breathe a few times and wait considerably longer. The crew came to me and said, "His family wants to have a witch doctor* treat him. Would you be willing?"

"What is it they want the witch doctor to do?" I asked.

"They want him to take a chicken and rub the man with it head to foot."

"Will it hurt the chicken?"

"It won't hurt the chicken," they said, "you can be sure, for that chicken will be the fee the witch doctor will get."

So I said, "All right, tell them he can do it if I can stand alongside and watch what he does."

Presently the witch doctor arrived with the chicken and a lot of relatives of the old man. They all stood around the bed and I had a front row space so that I could see what was happening.

---

* "The term leech is preferred for a man who treats physical ailments, in contrast to diviners, soothsayers, and magicians whose skills verge on the occult... My husband avoided the term witch-doctor [sic].... The leeches we knew...were modest unpretentious men who went about their doctoring without fanfare."
— *Winifred J. Harley*

They pulled the covers off the old man and started with the top of his head and rubbed him down as though with a washcloth, the chicken squawking to high heaven meantime. And rub they did. The assistant to the witch doctor stood alongside and said, over and over and over, throughout the whole performance, "Witch go out of him. Witch go out of him." So they rubbed him down to the points of his toes, flopped him over onto his stomach and did his back the same way.

That patient got well.

I've thought about that patient. I can't explain what happened, but I know that man was surrounded by family and friends who had complete faith that he would be healed.

Liberia was a very different experience from China. Ganta was about seven degrees north of the equator, where we could see both the North Star and the Southern Cross; but it was about 1,000 feet above sea level so that our days grew hot toward afternoon but were cool and comfortable mornings and evenings, and I was glad for two wool blankets at night. In December and January, for about two weeks, the dry harmatan wind blew down from the Sahara and caused rapid evaporation of any moisture left over from the rainy season. Later, in January and in February when the weather was dry, it was warmer, not terribly dry but more so than the rest of the year. The change to the rainy season always suggested the arrival of spring. We never realized how tired the trees and bushes looked until the rain gave everything a new and vivid green.

The people of Liberia were all very friendly. The Americo-Liberians, descendants of the freed slaves who founded the republic, were the wealthier and better-educated part of the population. They lived along the coast. In the hinterland were the country people, subdivided into various tribes, one of the greatest being the Mano, the tribe in our district. Socially somewhere between the Americo-Liberians who were largely Christians, and the country people who were mostly animists, were the Mandingos, who were mostly Muslims. A mixture with Arabs, they were often taller than the country people, with narrow bones, and were usually better-dressed. They were the traders of the area.

When Dr. George W. Harley and his wife, Winifred, founded the mission in 1926, the road to Ganta was a two-hundred-mile foot trail through the bush and it took six days to reach our village from the coast. Dr. Harley was a medical doctor, but as superintendent of Ganta Mission did very little medical work. His many other talents enriched the lives of the people in various ways. He imported vegetables and planted fields of pineapples, oranges and guavas. Mango trees lined both sides of the main road where it passed through the mission from Monrovia to Sanniquelie. Dr. Harley helped the District Commissioner, George Dunbar, build about fifty miles of this two-lane gravel road. During World War Two U.S. Army engineers completed it to the coast, cutting travel time to Monrovia to about seven hours.

Dr. Harley taught the people carpentry skills, how to make bricks and tiles and how to cut stone. With these skills they could make houses with stone foundations, beautiful beams and woodwork from the abundant mahogany trees, brick walls and tile roofs. These houses did not wash away in heavy rains as mud walls did, or catch fire from lightning so readily as those with thatch roofs. When I arrived at Ganta Mission in 1950, it included a school and dispensary at opposite ends of our clearing on the main road. There were also a machine shop and sawmill, the Harley's house and a small building, once the clinic, that served as storehouse and post office.

Two other couples, B.B. and Martha Cofield and Charles and Blanche Britt, lived across the half-mile clearing from me. They were evangelists and teachers. B.B. was also district superintendent, treasurer, postmaster; and he worked with Dr. Harley on construction projects as well. Winifred Harley was bookkeeper and turned her hand to many other jobs. Doretha Brown was in charge of the Girls' Hostel, no small job, and Mildred Black was doing literacy and language work. Later, when we had a school of nursing, Mildred taught English to the nurses.

At right angles to the big road, which ran north and south, was a driveway bordered with beautiful palms. I lived there with Mildred Black and our one nurse, Dagmar Petersen, a Danish-American who also had been with a mission in China. Our house was red-tan brick a story and an attic high, that had a roof of the beautiful tiles made at the mission. The palm trees around our house were festooned with many kinds of ferns and orchids and flowering vines, some full of large, lemon-yellow trumpet flowers. Close to the house were high shrubs of scarlet hibiscus.

When I was a child, somebody showed me a staghorn fern, and I thought it would be the height of all possible elegance to own one. Across from our house, in a space that had just been cleared for an athletic field, palm trunks covered with staghorn ferns lay on the ground. Each fern was big as a bushel basket. How utterly marvelous. I took an ax and chopped off some of these giant ferns and nailed them up on the palms near our house.

From the front of our house we looked across the new clearing for the athletic field out a hundred feet to where the clearing ended in jungle. On the field were four *bugabug* houses, as the termite hills were called, five or six feet high and yet to be leveled.

To the south of us beyond the school was the jungle again, with paths leading to some villages. Between the trees we could look out across a dip to a plain and another hill beyond, and knew that it went on and on like that across Africa: plains and hills, with little villages in their clearings in the bush.

The villages looked so exactly like the ones in the movies that I had to keep reminding myself they were real. The houses were made of round walls of clay, extended outwards at the bottom to make a porch a couple of feet wide where people sat under the low-thatch eaves. No windows. A door so low that even I had to stoop considerably to enter. Inside was dark, but one looked up through a loose framework of sticks that served as ceiling, the inside of a high, conical palm-thatch roof. Each family had several of these small huts to make up their compound. Some would have clay platforms against the wall for sleeping; spread with matting they

4

looked quite comfortable. In this polygamous society each wife had her own home.

A fireplace was in the middle of the floor, with three rocks to support an iron kettle, but most of the cooking was done outside and the fire inside was to heat the home at night. There was no chimney, but smoke made its way up, discouraging to some extent lesser inhabitants in the thatch and helping to preserve it. Walls were of mud and sticks, and to build a house sticks were placed standing in a circle, held in place by vines. The children danced in mudholes to mix mud with cow manure, while a drum beat a happy rhythm, and it was a great day when all was ready for the people to throw mud at the circle of sticks and smooth it down for the walls.

Some of the larger houses had partly walled-in porches outside the main house. And along the main street some of the houses even had windows with curtains. The spaces between the houses were hard, like a tennis court. Most villages were divided into quarters. In each quarter was its palaver kitchen, built like the other houses but larger and with no side walls, used for village gatherings.

There was a truck at Ganta Mission when I got there, a truck that the Harleys took to Ganta before there was a road. Dr. Harley needed a pickup to help him get in logs for his sawmill and building program, so in 1938 when he and Winifred with their eight-year-old son, Eugene, returned from a furlough, they took along their own Ford sedan.

There was no fine harbor at Monrovia then, and the ship had to anchor outside the sandbars. The Harleys, and Mildred Black who was with them, climbed over the rail into a glorified rowboat called a surfboat, and the Ford was lowered into another surfboat. Dr. Harley's idea was to ask the Firestone Plantation near Monrovia to put a pickup body on his sedan.

The Firestone people said they could use the Ford and swapped it for a pickup truck, which the Harleys drove the first fifty miles of road toward Ganta. The road ended in jungle and the truck had to be dismantled and headloaded the rest of the way. They had about a hundred carriers for the truck, all their luggage and hammocks, and it took a week to reach Ganta, creating a great stir in the villages along the way among people who had never seen a car before, nor so many white people.

Some money, which had been in the Methodist Board treasury for the use of Wuhu hospital, was transferred to Ganta when I arrived, to be used for medical work. We combined this with other donations and got a Jeep station wagon with four-wheel drive. A pretty dark maroon and a joy to drive, the Jeep was christened *I Lu Ping An,* which in Chinese means, "May you have a peaceful journey all the way."

There were no wars on in Ganta, so our journeys were peaceful, but hardly smooth, and I Lu Ping An lasted only three years. One bad-road trip was one that Mildred and I took to Bahn for a weekend with friends. Bahn was said to be about thirty-six miles further back in the bush, but the road seemed several times that distance. It took careful driving with one of us walking ahead and directing the other between the holes. As the holes were full of water I took along a stick to take soundings and to find out the nature of their bottoms. Once I jumped to an island in the middle of a pool and had to wait there until the car came alongside to pick me off.

We had no one to depend on in emergencies except ourselves. One night the plank house at the sawmill caught fire. That was the drying house where our lumber was seasoned by a continuous draught of warm air from a fire built outside in what looked like the entrance to an igloo. I grabbed the big copper fire extinguisher from our house, and the cook and I ran for the Jeep to race over to the fire. While Teacher Johma, who taught the boys carpentry, played the stream from our fire extinguisher on the fire, people converged from various directions. Then I remembered that in a recent drug order a worm-medicine item had been mistakenly filled with carbon tetrachloride cleaning fluid, and rushed over to our storeroom for that, as it was the same as the liquid in pyrene fire extinguishers. Our house also contributed an ax to chop up floor boards, and a bucket of water. Of course everybody else brought similar items and with our combined efforts the fire was stopped before it reached the seasoning lumber itself.

Life along the coast of Liberia was much like that in Europe, and Monrovia was our lifeline to the rest of the world. Mail came marked "via Monrovia," or we didn't get it at all. Postal delivery was an unknown luxury, even in Monrovia, and in the bush it arrived by truck once every few weeks, on no known schedule. Mail going and coming usually depended on somebody happening to go to Monrovia or on travelers passing through from further inland who had handfuls of mail thrust at them from every mission to carry along. For messages sent from one village to another, we depended on a runner, who usually walked, carrying a letter fastened to the split of a stick. He carried it to the first village, where that village's *tatua* man carried it on to the next, and so on in relays.

Tinned goods and other American food we ordered from the U.S. Trading Company at Firestone. But some things we asked family and friends to send us. I hadn't been in Ganta long when I wanted a good trowel for a garden, and clippers. There was a bushy lot of purple thumbergia growing close to our house that furnished too much snake-harbor. I also asked for a sturdy eggbeater, as ours went to pieces quickly beating up powdered into liquid milk every day.

I liked the bush, but after years in China it was strange to be with people whose mental processes I didn't follow. It usually helps to understand how people think if you understand their religion. There were no temples or wayside shrines or incense, so one day I asked one of the boys who helped at our clinic what they worshipped. He said it was a *thing* they fashioned out of wood. They would offer food to the *thing,* ask it a question and then throw down the split halves of a kola nut. If these halves landed with the same side up, the *thing* agreed; with different sides up, it disagreed. Exactly this same procedure, with halves of a dried bamboo shoot, was used in China, so I felt there was a true connection. I asked if this thing had the power to give the right answers, and he replied, "O yes!" When I asked how a thing a man made could know more than a man, he said he couldn't figure that out. Then he said that the "*thing* sometimes tells lies," not that it didn't know, but that it lied.

Later I learned the boy was talking about a *Meh,* a small face carved out of wood given to the young men when they were in the Bush School of the Poro Society, a big secret society whose head was known as The Big Devil. Women were not allowed to see it. Its spirit was understood to carry messages to *Wala,* whom they worshipped as creator of the universe. They did not pray directly to *Wala,* for they believed he was far too busy to listen to individuals. They trusted spirits who had direct access to *Wala,* and everything had a spirit: trees, rocks, animals, the *Meh,* even some people and especially their ancestors. When a family had a problem, or if something good happened, like the birth of a baby, they would go to some designated place, a big rock or tree or hill, taking with them a chicken or goat. The head of the family would call the names of important family ancestors, and when he thought enough had assembled, told the ancestors the family loved them and trusted them to tell *Wala* about their good fortune or their trouble. He said they brought this meat, which had been killed and would be cooking by this time in a pot sitting on three stones. The ancestors were expected to eat their part, the spirit part, while the family enjoyed the meal.

A Paramount Chief with R. L. Embree, President of the College of West Africa in Monrovia, who accompanied George and Winifred Harley on their first trek from Monrovia to Ganta in 1926.
Photo courtesy of Eugene L. Harley

Blacksmith Dow and his father. "The Mano blacksmith was 'a mighty man' in his village," wrote Winifred Harley. "He made iron tools as well as many wooden articles and iron objects used in the rituals of the [Poro] secret society. He stored in his loft those things which it is forbidden to see." Blacksmith Dow was a special friend to the Harleys throughout their years at Ganta. Accompanying a friend for a short distance at the start of a journey is called "carrying him" in Liberia. As the Harleys set out on the trail to start homeward for their 1930 furlough, Dow "carried" his friends and their three children a full day longer than anyone else.
Photo courtesy of Eugene L. Harley

First Ganta Mission residence, where the Harleys lived for ten years, being re-thatched in the 1930s. George Harley is perched, far right, at the peak of the ridge pole.
Photo courtesy of Eugene L. Harley

George Harley at the brickyard. "He believed that work with tools teaches integrity," wrote Winifred Harley. "If a joint fits, it fits; and if it doesn't, you can see it doesn't!"

Photo courtesy of Eugene L. Harley

George Harley turning a chair leg at the furniture shop. Winifred Harley wrote, "Most of the men who worked here were trained on the spot [by George Harley]. They turned out all kinds of furniture and equipment for the buildings on the mission, and outsiders always wanted many articles. President Barclay ordered a set of dining room furniture, and Dr. Harley took great pride in the fine chairs and table that our workmen made for him."

Photo courtesy of Eugene L. Harley

For thirty-five years Winifred Harley registered and questioned patients, took notes, trained a man to dress ulcers, handled fees, ran the still for distilled water; gave injections for yaws, leprosy and sleeping sickness, intravenous injections for schistosomiasis, and vaccinations for smallpox. A botanist of distinction, she published numerous articles, discovered a previously unknown fern (Ctenopteris punctata). Her specimens are at The Harvard University Gray Herbarium, with duplicates of many at Kew and the British Museum, and a few in the United States National Herbarium. These three collections, together with others that had been placed in herbaria over the previous 250 years, furnished the basis for her listing of The Ferns of Liberia, published by The Gray Herbarium in 1955.

Photo courtesy of Eugene L. Harley

George and Winifred Harley, about 1929, with Robert and infant Charles. At the age of four, Charles died tragically of accidental poisoning when he found quinine in the form of chocolate candy.
Photo courtesy of Eugene L. Harley

Eugene L. Harley, now a family internist in Atlanta, when he was eleven, with his .22 and a heron. "I can't believe now I would kill such a lovely bird," he writes. But at that time the Mano people had so great a hunger for meat that they used the same word to mean "animal" and "meat." Young Gene inevitably absorbed that view.
Photo courtesy of Eugene L. Harley

George Harley with sons Robert and Eugene. All three Harley boys were born at Ganta. Dr. Harley's wide-ranging curiosity led to careful studies and wide acclaim. As Bishop Ralph E. Dodge wrote in 1973, introducing Winifred Harley's book about Ganta Mission, "George W. Harley is a legend in the West African country of Liberia, in the Methodist Board of Missions, in North Carolina whence George came, and in anthropological circles. ...[he] was honored by his church, by universities, and by nations for his original research and creative touch; for his knowledge, and the humanitarian way in which he put it to use."

A Lot of Medical Work to be Done

One thing I did understand was that there was a lot of medical work to be done. We had only a dispensary when I arrived, and there we saw mothers with sick babies and children in the mornings, long lines of adults in the afternoons. We did minor surgery and soon had four in-patients stuck into corners of the dispensary, very much underfoot, and it was a comfort to know that early ambulation was now approved.

When we arrived each day at the clinic, a tall, post-operative Mandingo greeted us with upraised hands and a joyous "Allah be praised," and called down blessings on us. Another patient, an old Mano man, startled me one day by asking, "I have a song; may I sing it?" Then he jumped out of bed and danced gracefully up and down singing victory songs of warriors from ancient days.

Sores and ulcers were more easily healed than the prevailing tropical diseases, which included yaws, hookworm, trypanosomiasis (African sleeping sickness), two kinds of schistosomiasis, everyday malaria, amoebic dysentery, and noma, a disease that ate away parts of the face. We also had two different kinds of smallpox all year long, one very bad kind and one mild.

The children, so attractive in their bright garments, kinky hair, big eyes and bewitching smiles, had all the adult diseases plus whooping cough, measles, pneumonia, skin diseases and burns from falling into the fire or hot water.

When I returned to visit Ganta in 1978, there was no more smallpox in the country. I asked Dr. Wilfred Boayue, who had studied with me as a boy and was then a doctor back in Liberia, "How did you get rid of smallpox?" "We vaccinated every soul in the country," he said, "no one got away with an excuse." In 1962 volunteer doctors called Brother's Brother, vaccinated 200,000 people and trained Liberian aids to carry the campaign to the interior.

Wilfred Boayue was the son of Chief Charlie Boayue* of Bunadi, a village about thirty-five miles from Ganta. The chief had many wives and children. Wilfred, whose name was Sei Punagbea Boayue, got yaws when he was about eight years old and was very sick, but no one paid much attention to him. The yaws was in his elbow so that he could not bend his arm and it wasn't much use to him. One of our Liberian pastors visited this village and asked the chief when he left if he could take Sei Punagbea to our mission to see if anything could be done about the arm. "Take him along," said the chief, "he's no use to us."

So the pastor brought Sei Punagbea Boayue to Ganta Mission, and long afterwards Sei Punagbea told me that what impressed him most and made him sure that something special was about to happen was that on the way, whenever they came to a place where they could get water, the pastor made sure the boy drank first before he did. No one had ever done that before.

After he was well, Sei Punagbea stayed on to go to our school, and we taught him to work in our laboratory after school to pay his way. He managed to do his work with one straight arm. After a time he asked me to give him a foreign name, and I suggested Wilfred. He wanted to know if there had been a man named Wilfred, and "was he a good man?" So I told him the story of Wilfred Grenfell, the missionary to Labrador.

Wilfred got more and more interested in our medical work and wanted to be a doctor. I said he could be an internist, but he wanted to be a surgeon too, and was sure I could operate on his arm so that he could bend it. I said, "I've done that operation before, but I can't do it in Ganta. It must be done where everything is sure to

---

* The Boayues are an outstanding family. One of Chief Boayue's sons became an engineer, another was Liberia's Minister of Education but died in an auto accident in the 1960s. Wilfred is at present with the World Health Organization in Lusaka, Zambia. Two of his daughters are physicians, one an ophthalmologist in Kenya and one now in residency in St. Louis. Wilfred's brother Charles lives in Detroit with his son Charles, Jr., who is a minister. — *Eugene L. Harley*

be sterile. Someday you can have that operation and have a move-able arm, and then you can be a surgeon."

One of the young missionaries at Monrovia got students at the University of West Virginia to raise a scholarship for him. He went to America where he had the surgery he needed, then went on to college and medical school and became a surgeon. I met him in America and asked him, "How far can you bend your arm now?" He started to bend it and I thought, "that's all." But he kept on until it was bent straight up. "Is that enough?" he asked. When he returned to Liberia the government wanted to make him head of the Department of Health. But he wanted to return to Ganta, which he did for awhile, but they really needed him for bigger things and he finally accepted. Today Dr. Boayue works with the World Health Organization.

The most disheartening feature of the work when I arrived was the appalling dearth of trained native personnel. There was only one qualified Liberian doctor in Liberia, Dr. Togba, who was in charge of all the medical work in the country. Another had about finished his course in America and was soon expected back, but all the practicing doctors at the struggling government hospital were from other countries. There was no medical school, and no school that would qualify a student for entrance into a good medical school in America.

The situation for nurses was nearly as bad. The Firestone Hospital near Monrovia was training a class in 1950, and the U.S. Public Health people in Monrovia were also training a group. But on our stations we missionaries had to perform a great many tasks that in China were done by our Chinese nurses and technicians. In Liberia, when we did delegate work, we had to give close, detailed supervision.

Our Liberian neighbors were of the bush, and we could feel the culture of the bush in their courtesy. But the kind of back-ground needed to train them in modern medical work was far different from anything they had experienced, and we were told by old-timers that we were trying to jump centuries in a few weeks and to be patient.

By September 1950 an operating room had been built, and we

did a lot of minor surgery but held off on major for lack of space to put patients, and lack of crew to care for them. A new building, which would take up to thirty patients, was growing, but just how we would staff it we didn't know.

We started a teaching program to train a crew. Dagmar taught nursing procedures while my classes were in simple hygiene for the schoolboys and orderlies, community hygiene for older boys, English for the smaller boys and orderlies, care of patients for the orderlies, and simple physiology for the schoolboys. There were no pupil nurses yet, although some of our boys would have credits toward nursing once they had enough schoolwork to qualify and we began a nursing course. Our best stand-in was a Gold Coast man who had served three years as an orderly with the British Army medical people in India during the war. He became my operating assistant and did very well.

Without wards, many of our patients lived in a "sick-village" nearby, and walked or were carried in hammocks to us for treatment. In time we had two sick-villages of several thatch-roofed round mud houses where patients could live with their families. One was known as Gio Sick Town, because its people were of the Gio tribe, many of them with sleeping sickness. Its real name was *Ton leh we,* or Under The Palm Leaves.

Over the next several years a number of medical missionaries were added to our services, extra help that meant the work wasn't so crippled when one of us came down with bronchitis, hepatitis or dengue fever as when there was only one person to hold the fort.

Besides the clinic patients we had more than four hundred in a leprosy colony about a mile from the mission in a clearing among banana, orange and palm trees, with small round huts for residents. Many had open sores, some were minus fingers, toes, ears or noses, but few were privileged to have only leprosy. Malaria, schistosomiasis, sleeping sickness, dysentery, yaws and hookworm were known to all crowd into a single individual who had real reason to wonder what sort of witch had caught him. A few of the leprosy patients had been trained to change dressings and to give injections.

When I first went to the leprosy colony, a man blew his deer-horn trumpet to summon the patients to an open assembly-porch. Then a jolly group of men, women and children led us about to show us their water supply, which was a small sluggish stream, and people working at various crafts. Some wove mats with raffia, others wove purses and rugs. One man with fingers off at the second joint wove country cloth in long strips four inches wide. Others sewed the strips together to make very attractive garments and cot covers. An old fellow, who enjoyed the title of "tyrant," sat on a six-inch-high stool looking very important. His long gray whiskers were in four fuzzy braids. He smiled when we admired them.

We had frequent shooting accidents: often someone came in more or less peppered with shot as the result of another hunter "mistaking him for meat."* I remarked that I didn't see how so many hunters could mistake a man for meat, and was told that, "They don't make a mistake. They really do see an animal." The explanation was that a man who was a witch could change at will into an animal. It was the hunter's mistake to take for meat a man who had temporarily changed shape. When wounded, the meat immediately changed back into a man, and was brought to our hospital. So anyone who made the mistake of being shot immediately fell under suspicion of being a witch, whereas the man who shot him would of course be sued, but in the minds of the people had an excellent excuse.

One man came in bearing a letter from his tribal chief. It introduced the man and said he had been accused of "having a dreadful disease which is called Fate." The patient was bringing a lawsuit for defamation of character against the man who made the accusation, and I was called on to decide whether he really had the disease and if other people could catch it from him. Feeling a bit like Solomon, I declared that yes, indeed he did have Fate, but that nobody could catch it from him because they all had it but probably hadn't noticed it yet.

An emergency call took us to the Leprosy Colony for a woman who had gone crazy from a combination of sleeping sickness and

---

* The Mano hunger for meat was revealed in the word *wee,* which meant both "meat" and "animal."

18

malignant malaria. She thought she was a leopard and had been bewitching her friends. She had run out into the bush to live as a leopard, and when brought back by friends had rolled about over a cooking fire. We found her anchored by a strong vine, one end tied about her waist and the other around a pillar of the palaver house. By car lights we loaded syringes and quieted her with injections so that we could dress her burns. Then she drifted off to sleep and was carried into her house where her family sat down to watch over her by the light of the palm-oil flare. Treatments for sleeping sickness and malaria continued and she recovered.

One of the patients we were particularly interested in was a little Mandingo boy named Mamadi, brought in on a bicycle with his father walking alongside. We found eleven things the matter with him. He was swollen all over and could hardly see. We set to work, and in a few weeks Mamadi walked to our clinic himself and looked entirely different, with a normally-shaped face and cheerful smile. He was headed in the right direction with the prospect of a long and reasonably happy life, but wasn't yet well and wouldn't be for months.

Mamadi was in such bad shape when he came to us because his father had been away for some months, and the women of that tribe did particularly badly about caring for the children. According to their Muslim ideas, being women they had no souls and were not worth educating. They didn't go about and exchange ideas the way women of non-Muslim tribes did, and the children suffered. It wasn't the women's fault; they hadn't a chance to learn how to care for them. So I started a campaign to get across to the Mandingo men the idea that they would never have healthy and well-cared-for sons until they started to educate their girls. An old priest, whose daughter was my first obstetrics patient, agreed to the reasonableness of the idea, but it was a new idea and would take a long time before anything would be done about it.

One of the first people I met in Ganta was an unhappy looking old lady everybody called Grandma. She was in pain most of the time from a severe yaws infection of the right shin bone. I knew that one day, if she put her weight on it, it would break, and begged her to let me take the leg off as the disease was so far gone there was no curing it. But she said no.

One day I found Grandma sitting on the ground crying. The leg had finally broken, and she reluctantly let me take the leg off. I thought she would be better and happier without the pain. But she wasn't. She had been walking with a homemade crutch, but without the leg she didn't even try to walk. She just sat and cried.

One evening a European doctor who was visiting us while doing some government health work, listened to my story about Grandma. Now this doctor had lost a leg and had a splendid artificial one. He always wore shorts, so all the mechanism at the knee was visible, and people loved to gather round and watch him walk. I said, "Would you be willing to show your leg to Grandma? Her son is in our construction department, and could make a leg for her."

The doctor agreed, and over to Grandma's house we went and he sat down beside her and showed her his leg. She looked at it in amazement, but he realized she didn't know it was artificial. So he took it off. She was startled, but still, to her it was just something strange that foreigners do. We explained that she could have one like it, but she said she didn't want one. Then the doctor said, "She doesn't realize yet that my stump is just like hers." So he took the sock off his stump and showed her it was the same length and shape as hers. But the idea didn't seem to get across.

When he was about to leave, suddenly I had an idea. "Doctor," I said, "since you've been so kind, would you be willing to do one more thing? Would you be willing to dance a few steps, just to show her how beautifully you can use that leg?"

"I'd be delighted," he said, "but only if I can dance with you!" Well, that was something. When you grow up in a Methodist parsonage you don't learn to dance. Furthermore, the floor of that room was made up of boards of uneven thickness, uneven lengths, and there was no smooth space. But we tried. Then the doctor said goodnight and went his way and I returned home.

Grandma had not smiled, had not looked pleased, had not looked even interested. She just sat and looked broken-hearted. But a day or two later Grandma's granddaughter came to me and said, "What do you think! Grandma is laughing! She hasn't laughed for years. She sits and looks sad, and then suddenly she remembers you and the doctor trying to dance and she laughs and laughs!"

Grandma never agreed to an artificial leg, but she did start to walk again with her old wooden crutch.

Many unexpected things happened when people came to our clinic. One man came in for an operation, looked at our little space for patients and exclaimed, "What? The house big so?" and ran away. More than a year later he returned, having screwed up his courage. We told him the ward had not grown any smaller, but he stayed and had his operation and recovered well.

Another man came in with two moths the size of your thumb, which he said had come out of his ears. I asked him how many had come out in the last couple of years, and he promptly said, "twenty-two." He asked for medicine to keep the moths from flying out, and we started him on tryparsamide for sleeping sickness. At the village of Zor Zor, some time later, a woman brought me the same kind of moths that "came out of her head."

A woman arrived in whom we wanted to induce labor, so we rigged up an intravenous of pituitrin to run very, very slowly, about four drops a minute, even though diluted. Suddenly we heard her start to screech, and we went running. She said she was having terrible pains, and we found the drip running in a stream. The fellow who mopped the floor had seen people get intravenous medicine before and noticed how fast the drip usually came. So he tried to be helpful and opened the cock.

We did the first Caesareans done in our part of the country, and one was quite dramatic for there were twins. Caesareans became very popular, so that we had to discourage women perfectly capable of normal childbirth from having them. On one occasion a woman came in for a Caesarean who really needed it. It was at night and we had only a skeleton crew on duty. The husband wanted to watch, so I put him in a chair in a corner of the room and said, "You sit right there, and don't move from that chair."

We scrubbed up and I paid no attention to him, and all went well until we got to the point where we were about to pull out the baby. You make a small incision in the uterus and work the baby out gently. You don't want to heave it out as fast as you can, but the father decided we needed a strong man to do the job and ran over to pull. I yelled for help and someone on duty in the ward hauled him off and sat him down outside the operating room.

When I had been in Ganta a couple of years we had an outbreak of dog bites in several villages, and a lot of us had to have the Pasteur anti-rabies treatment. Mildred and I made two very hasty trips down to Monrovia to get the vaccine. The Government Bureau of Health radioed to the Pasteur Institute at Dakar for vaccine, and the Firestone Hospital doctors kept the radio busy hurrying it along. All sorts of people helped, including a Pan American aircraft official in Frankfurt, Germany, who relayed a message to Dakar that couldn't be got there directly. We went back down to the airport to receive the stuff when it came in from Dakar, and brought it upcountry in a Coca Cola cooler.

Ganta Village

Photo by Mildred A. Black

Ganta clinic

Photo by Mildred A. Black

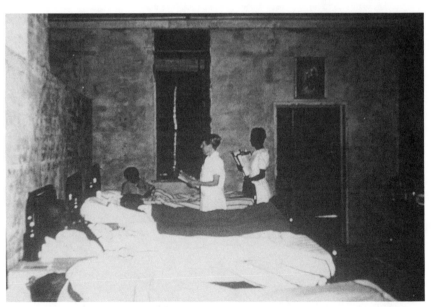

Hyla Doc on ward rounds

Photo courtesy of Eugene L. Harley

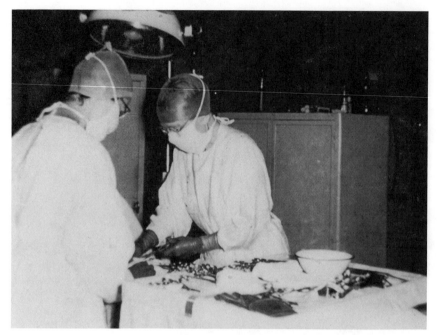

Hyla Doc operating

Photo by Mildred A. Black

Leprosy Village, Ganta Mission

Photo by Mildred A. Black

Monday Blegay at Ganta Mission School, is now a surgeon, Dr. Robert Blegay.
Photo by Mildred A. Black

Ganta ambulance

Photo by Mildred A. Black

Ganta ambulance

Photo by Mildred A. Black

Ganta ambulance

Photo by Mildred A. Black

Hyla Doc and Edgar Whitcomb visiting Wilfred Boayue in 1969 at the Methodist Church of Indiana. Edgar Whitcomb, former governor of Indiana, and Hyla Doc were interned by the Japanese in the same camp in Shanghai during 1942 and 1943.
Photo courtesy of Wilfred Boayue

Wilfred and Stella Boayue in 1984 with their children Simone, Nya Kwai, Paul Tiala and Wilfred, Jr.
Photo courtesy of Wilfred Boayue

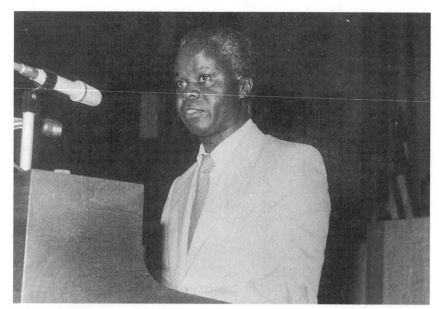

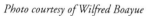

Wilfred Boayue addressing the Annual Meeting of the Liberia Medical and Dental Association as President, 1984.

Photo courtesy of Wilfred Boayue

Wilfred and Stella Boayue with their two younger boys in 1991. Wilfred, Jr. is at Virginia Technical School, Simone at Yale.

Photo courtesy of Wilfred Boayue

"Somebody Witched Me"

When I asked my patients what was wrong with them, their answer was usually, "Somebody witched me." To them the puzzle was to find the witch and some stronger medicine than the witch had.

The method of dealing with sickness in the bush villages was taken over by women who made a business of catching witches. They called themselves the Razor Society. Once they located a witch, their aim was to bring illness and death to the witch. One of my patients was a poor fellow who was accused by his fellow villagers of being the witch who caused illness in the village. When he got sick himself they thought he should go to the Razor Society to report his misdeeds and take his punishment. No one but a couple of Christians believed him when he insisted he had not been doing any witchcraft, and they brought him to us. The village chief had tied him up and fastened to him a big piece of timber so that he couldn't run around and bother people, but even in his foggiest moments he held to the belief that he was not a witch. We treated him for sleeping sickness, and after a bit he lost the foggy look, stopped being noisy and troublesome, and finally recovered completely.

One little girl from Dinamu who was very sick with malignant malaria was also supposed to be a witch. We managed to get her back to health and thought we had the family convinced and the Razor Society discredited. But a few days after the first episode, the family brought her back to us in the middle of the night, sicker than before with alternating delirium and convulsions from malignant malaria. We did all we could, but couldn't bring her out of it, and she died at four in the morning. All members of the family were obviously afraid of her, and no one cried when she died. Usually there was loud wailing to mourn a death, but when a witch died nobody cried. Her death seemed to prove to the family that the Razor Society was right after all.

Another patient was a young boy, Sei Yekese, who had tetanus. For him to recover meant more than saving his life, for the Razor Society had decreed that he was a witch and doomed. We had a time trying to keep the family from taking him out of the hospital and turning him over to the Society, for the family was afraid of "witch palaver." We even quoted the president of the country to them, for he was much opposed to the Razor Society. And we quoted the District Commissioner, who wrote a letter to Dr. Harley saying that the boy was by no means to leave the hospital until after recovery. Fortunately we had some tetanus antitoxin on hand, and Dagmar went down to Monrovia to get more from the U.S. Public Health Service. Dagmar packed it in cold thermos containers and sent it back to Ganta by a special messenger. There were bridges out, and he had to walk part way, but he got through in one long day, and within a few minutes after he reached us we got another dose of the blessed stuff into Sei Yekese, and he did recover.

But that Razor Society and all the talk of witches caused much trouble. One day Dr. Harley did a very brave act to discredit them. We had gone for a hike and left our truck at a village before setting out on foot. When we returned for the truck we learned there had been an outbreak of measles in the village, and two boys had died of it. The Razor Society had prepared some rites to determine who was the witch who was killing their children. They had a huge pan filled with cooked rice. All the villagers were gathered around the bowl, and when we arrived were about to each eat a mouthful of rice. The first person to get sick after that would be the witch.

The chief was worried. The two children who had died were in his own family, and he was aware that measles could hit anybody in the village. Dr. Harley asked if he couldn't intervene. But he said he could not. So Dr. Harley stood up and made a speech.

"This rice," he said, "is so-so country rice with no magic in it. If everybody eats it, somebody will be picked as witch who isn't a witch at all." Then he asked the chief to destroy the rice, but the chief wouldn't touch it.

"Well," said Dr. Harley, "then I will." And he picked up the huge pan of rice and held it up and said, "I will dump this rice out on the ground, and you will see that nothing happens." And he did. The people were frightened, but Dr. Harley said, "See? Nothing happens. Nothing but so-so country rice. We will come tomorrow with medicines and hold a clinic here. Anybody who gets sick, we will treat him and help him get well."

Dr. Harley was a brave man, because he knew somebody could put poison in his food to prove him wrong. But everybody loved Dr. Harley, and no one tried to poison him.

That Razor Society also made a lot of trouble over at the Leprosy Colony. People from the colony kept coming to us and asking if we could stop them. I didn't know what to do to stop this powerful group of women, so at the mission we talked it all over. Finally B.B. Cofield went to see the District Commissioner and asked him if there was any way to stop them. "Have you any evidence of what they do that you can show me?" he asked.

"No," said B.B., "but I'll get some."

So B.B. waited until a time when a fringed fence made of grasses and reeds was hung across the main path to the Leprosy Colony. This meant that the Razor Society was having a meeting and no one who was not a member should go through this fence on pain of death.

B.B. got one of the Liberian pastors, a man he had worked with for many years, to break through that fence with him. When they appeared, the Razor Society women shrieked, disappeared into the jungle and left behind all their instruments of torture. B.B. scooped them up in a basket and he and the pastor took them to the commissioner. "That's fine," said the official, "now we can do something. But be careful. Those women are well-trained in the use of poison, you know."

B.B. told his cook what he had done and added, "If I die in the next couple of weeks, well, everybody knows that you are my cook."

The cook told him, "Don't eat anything at anybody else's house, eat only what I cook for you. The things I cook, I know it. What somebody else cooks, we don't know. You will be safe."

The head of the Razor Society hitched a ride on a truck going upcountry and barged into the office of the official and said, "I bring a complaint against B.B. Cofield. He has stolen my things."

The commissioner showed her the basket and asked, "Are these your things?"

"Yes," she said, "those are my things. B.B. Cofield stole them."

The commissioner said she couldn't have them because she was using them to harm people.

"But my mother gave them to me," she insisted, "they are my personal possessions." They talked about it at length and finally the official agreed to give them back to her if she would promise to send them far away and never use them or have another meeting of the Razor Society again.

She promised, and she kept her promise. Several years later she was discharged from the Leprosy Colony and decided to take the God palaver seriously.

Our leprosy treatment was so successful that by the time I left Liberia that village of 400 had grown to 1200 people. I was upset and asked Dr. Harley, "Can't the government send some of them somewhere else?"

Dr. Harley said, "If I had leprosy, I would crawl on my hands and knees to get to Ganta's Leprosy Village." Finally we worked out a system so that people with leprosy beyond the contagious stage could live in other villages, and every week we made a round of the villages to see them.

B.B. and Martha Cofield in 1950s with the daughter of Griff Davis, the young photographer with USAID who took this picture. Martha taught in the Ganta School.
Photo courtesy of Martha Cofield

B.B. Cofield, Liberia Annual Conference Treasurer, on a construction site in the 1950s. Winifred wrote of B.B. that "he began at once [1941] to shoulder much of the mechanical routine of the growing station. He had a positive genius for carrying on several projects at the same time, never losing sight of the end result in a forest of details. Whatever he might be doing he did it with a smile. Although his first aim was to do pastoral work, the day-by-day activity and maintenance almost swallowed him up for a while, much as it had Dr. Harley."
Photo courtesy of Martha Cofield

Movie night, 1950s, Ganta School, open to the public with B. B. Cofield as projector operator.

Photo courtesy of Martha Cofield

B. B., Martha and eight-year-old Bonnie, furlough 1949.

Photo courtesy of Martha Cofield

God and Boiled Drinking Water

I had to have an interpreter with me, but began to pick up words and phrases of the Mano language. The official language of Liberia was English, but in the villages a great number of tribal languages were spoken. Until Mildred Black arrived, no one, foreigner or native, had ever tried to write or read these languages. It bothered Mildred to be unable to understand her students or speak to them in their own language. So she decided to learn the major language, Mano, and to devise a written script. The villagers were surprised to find there was a way for them to correspond. It was like magic. But they worked their farms during the days and were afraid to go out at night, so the only way Mildred had to teach them to write and read their own language was to go out to the villages at night.

In one she found an older lady who was very intelligent. Ma Vonyi wanted to learn to read, so every night they had a class together and other villagers gathered to listen. Soon they wanted to learn too, so Mildred taught Ma Vonyi how to teach them. On her furlough in 1950 Mildred worked out a series of language lessons for foreigners. After she returned we got systematic and guided language work for the first time, using her lessons which she completed as we went along, keeping a few lessons ahead of us. Each of us had a Mano "informant" at our elbow as we studied, to make sure we used correct pronunciation, tones and idioms.

In the middle of each session we would go to one of the nearby villages to practice conversation. The people knew we were studying their language and were pleased to talk with us, especially about what they were doing.

One day a potter lady at Gbaishello gave us a demonstration of her pot-making. She started with a mass of wet clay, and to my surprise made the wall of the pot first, without any bottom. She built it up of sausage-like rolls of clay added one by one and rubbed together. Instead of using a wheel, she built the clay on a small piece of matting, and turned that around with her hand as she worked, smoothing the inner and outer surfaces with rounded pieces of gourd-shell. She told us that after the pot had dried and hardened a little she would turn it over and add the bottom. Then she would oil it before adding a design with carved bracelets or a ridged seashell. After that the pots got put up on the stick framework, which served as ceiling in her house, to dry by the heat of the cooking fire before she baked them in an outdoor kiln.

There was a woman potter in Dinamu who was my friend. She made her pots the same way. Visitors to Dinamu, who had not been there before, would want to buy her pots, but sometimes she didn't have any ready to sell. So I said, "Why don't you make up a lot of pots and I will buy them from you. Then when people want them I will sell the pots to them." She thought this was a good idea and would send pots to Ganta and tell the person who brought them to tell me that they were from my friend. She never gave her name, just called me her friend. So for several years all the space under my bed was filled with pots. They were very popular with Ganta visitors.

The village people used a vivid local idiom to speak to us that I enjoyed very much. They spoke of new converts to Christianity as "those who have turned their hearts," and baptized people were "those inside God's fence." Church members were "those under God's roof."

In a school play a chief said, "If I send my son to the mission school, he will come back talking about God and boiled drinking water." We hoped he would.

One of our young teachers leading chapel told the story of Jacob in his own words: "Jacob was walking about and found a ladder up to heaven. At night he lay down and slept under the ladder, and dreamed of angels going up and down it, so he grabbed one and wrestled him all night. Near daybreak the angel said, 'Let me go,' because no angel can go walking about in the daytime. Jacob said, 'I will not let you go,' so the angel just gave him a good slap on the thigh and went on back to heaven."

Around Christmas one year, two American boys stayed with us who were in Liberia for some weeks in connection with map-making by aerial photography. They heard Mildred tell the Christmas story, first using Mano and then the English that the villagers used: "That King Herod was a proper rascal! ...Joseph and Mary couldn't get any place in the Stranger's House in that town, because the people were too plenty...God's messenger said, 'Don't be scared. The thing I come to tell you is fine so. There's a new pickin in David's Town, come to show all the people how God loves them. You must go there and see. And the shepherds looked at each other and said, 'Come. Let we go.'"

On the way home that night one of the boys said, "I've heard that story all my life, but it was never before so vivid."

Speaking of Christmas, we do well to remember that Christian people in Liberia, indeed throughout Africa, take pride in the fact that the Christ Child was given shelter in Egypt when he was in great danger from "that proper rascal, Herod."

Ganta choir, when services were held in the school's unfinished attic. Hyla Doc is in the back row, Martha Cofield at the pedal organ, and Bonnie Cofield barely visible in the front row.

Photo courtesy of Eugene L. Harley

On her retirement, Mildred Black was named Dame Grand Commander by the Republic of Liberia in recognition of her exceptional service to the Republic.

Of Lolos and Cobras, Owls and Chickens

The wildlife in Liberia was different from any I had known. We had one bird called the Pepper Bird, that sang early morning something that sounded like, "Red pepper, green pepper, sweet pepper tree." At noon, we were told, he flew to the guard of the king's treasure (what king wasn't specified, as Liberia was a republic) and asked, "Guard, guard, is all the king's property quite correct?" I told our cook I thought it strange that a bird up here in the bush should speak English, but he said, "Oh, no, monkeys speak English too." He explained that the small monkey goes out on the branch grabbing all the fruit saying, "Dat's mine! Dat's mine! Dat's mine!" But the big monkey shakes a disapproving finger at the little one and says, "No, no, individual!" meaning one for each, and nobody is to grab it all.

I had a ridiculous pet *lolo,* which was his Mano name. He was about ten inches long, his skin was scaly with very small scales and he changed color for he was a chameleon. He was pale green when asleep, and varied from green to black, sometimes having lengthwise white strips on the sides and sometimes most bizarre markings all over him in light and dark green, green and brown, or green and black, with or without the white stripes. His head was oversize, and flat like an armadillo's but more so. His eyes were large, spherical, and protruded from his head. Most of each eye was covered with scaly skin, leaving only a tiny aperture for each, that opened and closed. The two eyes moved independently, so he could look straight ahead with one and straight backward with the other, or straight up, at the same time. His four feet were split, with two-clawed toes fused in one half and three in the other, so that when stepping the foot was an inverted Y, and when standing an inverted T. He also had a firm grip when he brought his fingers together. All along his backbone to the tip of his tail was a row of small points like an iguana, and the tail curled up under him like a seahorse, only the whole of it curled. When he walked, which he did slowly, it stood out straight behind him, giving a ludicrous impression of frozen speed. When angry he opened his mouth wide, actually opening most of his head, disclosing a bright yellow interior, and made a noise like a cobra. That was probably why people were afraid of him, although his jaws had no teeth nor strength nor poison, and his bite was harmless except to insects. He stalked insects and caught them with a swift, long tongue, and also dug in the ground like a mole.

While I had him I would put him down on the lawn and some time later return and pick him up in about the same place. But one day he must have put on speed and disappeared. Somebody said he looked prehistoric, and somebody else said futuristic. All of us felt inclined to doubt there could be such an impossible animal.

One day we had a complicated skirmish that began with a snake falling out of a palm tree back of our house. People shouted and others came and found sticks and went into action. After variously losing and finding the snake and poking it out of hiding, our white-faced African duck meantime repeatedly getting into the midst of the picture and having to be shooed away, the snake was finally killed, a six-foot black cobra, shiny as a black mirror. The schoolboys carried him off in triumph to feast on later. Another day a seven-foot black cobra was killed a little way down the hill behind our house. In accordance with wise native custom, the head was chopped off and buried immediately. This reminded me of a patient who came into the clinic complaining of heart palpitation dating from a year before when he was bitten by a snake he met while up in the palm tree cutting bunches of palm nuts.

When the clinic crew heard that, they were amazed, and told me, "But the snakes never do that! They have a law that if they meet a man in a tree they never bite him until they get down to the ground." I asked the reason for that law, and they said, "When a man is up in a tree, he's already in danger. It isn't good to bite a man who is already in danger. That snake broke the law." I asked a number of other people about that, who all confirmed that snakes do have and follow such a law.

40

Anyway, this man killed the snake with the cutlass he had for cutting palm nuts, and never came down the palm until he had all his nuts. When I remarked that he was a brave man, Frank, our interpreter, said, "Ma, he's a Gipu man, and Gipu men are sassy. That's why the Government had such a hard time to conquer them in the wars. They made an arrow poison that was strong so! If they shot a man with that kind of arrow, he didn't die right away, but if he leaned against another man that one would die first and this one afterward."

One night a woman patient suddenly leaped out of bed screaming. Everybody came running to see what was the matter, and we found a hole in the ceiling directly over her bed. A rat had come down through the hole and dropped on the lady, and of course she was upset about it. In a few minutes we saw why the rat had come down, because a snake followed after and landed on the bed too.

On another occasion I was sitting out under a palm tree studying the language with a schoolboy to help me with my pronunciation when our cat came out. She snarled and spat at me and clawed at my shin and spoke horrible cat language all of which she had never done before. Then she jumped up on my lap and clawed at my face. I put her down and she jumped right back up again, so I said, "Well, let's stop language lessons. Maybe she didn't get her breakfast." I got up and was halfway back to the house to see to her food when the cat walked off quite calmly. About an hour later the schoolboys shot down out of the palm tree a very poisonous seven-foot mamba.

We always kept a gun handy for snakes. One of the boys was good at handling a gun. The boys would come running and say, "Please give us the gun, there's a snake out here." And I'd ask, "Who's going to handle that gun?" "Oh, so-and-so." "Well, tell him to come and get it." So he'd come get the gun and one cartridge, only one. When the snake was dead they'd cut it in sections and divide it up according to the number of people who had discovered it in the tree, and they'd all have some snake meat for lunch.

After this had gone on for a number of years I said, "Look, what we do is not fair. We give the gun, and give the cartridge, you get the meat. Where's our part?"

They said, "You want some?"

I said, "Of course! After this, every time you get a snake with our gun, you bring us our part, one foot of that snake is our part."

So they said, "You talk true, Ma, you talk true. We will." So they did. And we had snake each time they killed one. It was good, like fish.

But then we got a new missionary who wasn't used to such goings-on. Next time we had a snake there was no snake meat, and I asked our cook, "Where's the snake? We gave the gun. We gave the cartridge. No meat on the table."

"No." he said, "Sei got it this time."

I said, "You tell Sei he can have his part but not our part."

"All right."

But next time again there was no snake meat on the table and I asked the cook why not and he gave another excuse. The third time there was no meat I said, "Now you talk true. I want to know where's our part of that snake."

"Ma, I talk true. Ma Malone," that was the new missionary, "she say, the day snake meat come on this table she going to make war!"

"Well," I said, "we don't want war in this house. If palaver stands that way, let it be so."

We did have a number of snaky stories, but actually I was in Ganta for seven months before I ever saw a snake, and in all the time I was there I saw only about a half dozen cases of snakebite. And all of those recovered. We had more than a hundred boarding students and some day students going about barefoot, but only two were bitten, neither seriously. One said, "The snake wouldn't have bitten me, but I confused him by stepping on his tail."

One Christmas Dr. Harley gave me a tortoise about a foot and a half across. He lived on bananas and papaw, and walked much faster than the *lolos,* our white-faced duck following solemnly a couple of feet behind whenever he went for a stroll.

The schoolboys came in groups to call on the tortoise and scratch his back for him, and were disgusted with me when after a few days, seeing he wasn't happy in captivity, I let him go in the bush one evening so he could get away before they found him. They protested loudly, "But he be fine soup, sweet-o!" and went looking for him, without success. Everything living meant food to them: the termites, especially the fat termite queens, caterpillars, snakes, rats, everything.

Somebody caught an owl while it was asleep and brought it to the clinic to sell. I bought it for fifty cents and had much more than that amount of interest in it. It was finely-marked in brown, with enormous eyes that it shut one at a time. It had claws that made me wish for a heavy gauntlet such as falconers wear; but after I cut the tight cord that had tied its feet, it made no effort to grab my fingers with those claws, nor to bite me, though it snapped its beak loudly. After powdering it to kill its mites, I took it home and let it fly in our attic to catch the bushy-tailed squirrel-rats that lived there. They were dormice, such as *Alice in Wonderland* met. These dormice had been numerous and noisy after our cats left us for the bush, as many cats did there, except for a few days when bees preempted our attic. While the bees were there the dormice took a vacation, and when the owl came they did the same. After a few days the house boy opened the window shutters one afternoon and the owl flew away. That was all right with me, but that night the bushy-tailed tribe came back and celebrated all night.

One day some of the schoolboys came to us saying, "Your chicken has gone in a hole, and she won't come out." This was a very nice little native hen "dashed" to us by the chief of the village at the foot of Mt. Bili where we went for short holidays.

We asked, "Is she happy in the hole?"

"We don't think her heart can be satisfied," said the boys.

"But if she went in by herself, why doesn't she come out again?" we asked.

"Come look."

Our new laundry shed had hollow brick pillars, and seven or eight feet down in one of them was our Bili hen, making it very clear that her heart was not satisfied. How to get her out? I had a red bandanna handkerchief, so by tying three corners of it together and a string to the last corner, we let it down full of gravel and brick fragments. This we did many times until the hole filled and the chicken came up and out.

Now the little country hen was a scrawny thing as were all the country hens; it was not the custom to feed them. But she was a very good mother. So we sent for six eggs of big Rhode Island Reds, and she hatched three roosters that we called Winken, Blinken and Nod. Winken got run over by a truck and Blinken went to the chief of a nearby village. Nod we kept. We sent for twelve more eggs and our little Bili hen raised a lot of fine children, all considerably larger than their foster mother. The hens we kept to lay more eggs, while the roosters all became fathers of improved poultry in the villages. The sale of eggs and young cocks paid for the feed we bought for the flock, which increased to more than fifty. We couldn't have afforded to keep chickens on that scale otherwise. We did get a few eggs from country hens that we kept for hatching and bringing up thoroughbred children, since the thoroughbreds weren't as good at it. At one time a disease wiped out most of our flock, but we started over again.

One night we were awakened by squawking chickens and dashed out of the house to find our back yard alive with driver ants. Pajamas are not the correct garb to wear when you tackle flesh-eating drivers; they go up the legs and chew on you. We dashed back indoors for safer clothing, then as quickly as possible grabbed the chickens, brushed off the ants and put the complaining birds in the Jeep. Cofields had a chicken house so we took them there.

Christmas and Devils

Getting ready for my first Christmas in Ganta, we tried to find a tree in a land of no evergreens. We picked branches of various sorts but they all withered in a day or two. Finally we tried an ornamental tree that grew in all our dooryards. It had variegated green and yellow and red leaves and was slow to wither, so that was our clinic Christmas tree. For trimmings we saved up empty ampoules for weeks ahead and hung them, filled with red, green, yellow and blue-colored water, on the tree. For icicles we saved twisted strips of tin that we peeled off with a key when opening plasma cans. Winifred Harley brought out some wooden figures for a crèche. They had been carved at the mission years before, but the set was incomplete. Some of the clinic crew made the missing figures: one boy made a manger for the baby, two made shepherds, and I carved an angel from soap.

B.B. and Martha Cofield worked up a Christmas play given by the school boys, plus clinic crew plus a few others. My mandolin helped with the music and I helped train the choir and the three kings who were soloists. A feature I never saw before was a flash bulb set off when the angels appeared to the shepherds. This startled the audience as well as the shepherds, and made real the words, "Be not afraid." I suppose seeing angels would be even more startling. A lot of the town came to the play, sitting on benches in front of the school porch, which served as the stage.

Later in the night, the angels came caroling, each carrying a candle and a hymnbook. They came in when we opened the door and sang all the carols they knew before going on to Harley's. The clinic crew learned the carol of the friendly beasts, and loved it and saw no reason to stop singing it once Christmas was over.

It was fine to have the mandolin for Christmas music. It had given way in the fall, and I feared its music was finished, as it hadn't been up to rain forest humidity. That of the Yangtze Valley had already nearly done it in. But Dr. Harley was exceptionally clever at repairing things, and took it in hand. He strongly reinforced it inside, reglued it with African glue, made a new bridge, and behold it was better than it had ever been. I had never dared tune it up to pitch in warm or damp weather, but after that it took the pitch just fine.

My family sent me new strings for Mandy and a new pitch pipe. From the new strings I supplied my missing E string, and gave the others to an Irish missionary at a nearby station who had repaired my watch. He never let me or anyone else ever pay him. But he had a mandolin he had been unable to use for a long time for lack of strings, and he had nothing to tune by. So I gave him my pitch pipe too, as I could tune by my old friend the seabag lock, which vibrated in D and had served well in China.

In Ganta town nobody had a clock and hours meant nothing, nor months, since they didn't vary, nor years, since there's no winter or summer, and nobody knew how old they or their children were. So one Sunday afternoon when we went to the village of Kpain for a meeting, it was already in session on the front porch of one of the larger houses.

When we arrived, all the people rose up and shook hands with each of us, snapping fingers at the finish of each handshake. Then they sat down again on the floor, but brought chairs for us. Chiefs and honored guests rated chairs. A brother in a red-and-yellow loincloth and remnants of a brown tweed vest led the singing of some Mano hymns, which were partly antiphonal, with two groups overlapping. Some of the time people sang harmony with the parts following exactly parallel, like early European harmony. Sometimes they sang in a number of keys simultaneously, each person steadfastly carrying through in his own key without being confused by the others, rather a marvel. They were worth hearing. It was a new Christian group expressing in their own medium the new truths they had learned, and they sang joyfully. I sometimes wondered what it must be like to learn for the first time about a loving God. The whole group accompanied us back to the Jeep and made us a gift of bananas from their trees.

On our way home from that meeting, we saw a crowd with drums and stopped to watch a "country devil" doing a whirling dance. He came over to our Jeep to greet us through his spokesman, and seemed pleased that we had spotted his dance in the Jeep lights. We made a bargain with the devil and invited him to Ganta during Annual Conference to dance for the bishop and down-country missionaries who were our guests. This devil was called a Vai devil, from the Vai tribe and spoke only through his spokesman. He came at night, appearing out of the dark, and disappeared into it at the end of his dance, all to the eerie sound of drumming. An animated haystack five or six feet high, topped with a high head-dress, with no sign of face or arms or legs, he leaped and whirled about, or drifted without seeming effort from place to place, between times, settling down and acting exactly like a haystack. He would sometimes shake himself to the rhythm of the drums, or suddenly rush toward bystanders, who scampered out of his way, and at other times would whirl until the poor devil must have been very dizzy.

Mano devils, we learned had masks, could sing and talk through an interpreter, and they danced on stilts. We always tried to get a Mano devil to come visit us whenever the bishop visited.

Fallow Fields

Moses was right when he talked about the need for fields to lie fallow one year in seven, and on my arrival in Liberia I began a campaign to persuade African missionaries to take vacations. There seemed to me to be an obvious connection between the two facts that missionaries in Africa went on working without a break, and that Africa was called the graveyard of missionaries,

The term in Liberia was a short one, because of the climate, but it wasn't the climate that did them in, it was malaria and other diseases and lack of vacations. Many missionaries came to me in bad physical condition, but picked up when on strenuous urging they took time off. I wrote to the Board and learned that the policy for Africa called for periodic vacations, and at Annual Conference the bishops backed me up.*

So when an invitation came from Dr. and Mrs. Yung of Zor Zor to spend a couple of weeks with them and deliver their baby when it came due, I promptly accepted. A driver and Jeep came for me, and we set out for the border-crossing to French Guinea. After a genial stop at Liberian customs, where the staff were neighbors of ours and some of them our patients, we went on to the St. John's River, where the French and Liberian governments were constructing a bridge. Five trucks ahead of us waited for the ferry, a platform floated on empty boilers. It was chained to a steel cable and pushed across the river and back in slow motion by force of the current as the length of the bow and stern chains was adjusted.

---

* "Guard your health; nothing interferes with a man's lifework so much as his dying." Charles Willoughby's advice to the Harleys, Kennedy School of Missions in Hartford, CT.   — *Winifred J. Harley*

There were a lot of people waiting to cross. One young man, in some way connected with the ferry, sat in a hammock under a thatched shelter and played continuously on a guitar, slightly out of tune, a four-measure melody based on four chords and repeated four times. He played it over and over without interruption for nearly two hours. Remarkable to relate, it rather heightened the time of waiting. The banks of the river were high, except where the road approached it, and old trees overhung it at both sides.

Across the river at French Guinea customs, again we had a long wait, for the road beyond customs narrowed, and a lot of French trucks headed toward us were held up for customs clearance before boarding the ferry. The French customs commissioner was an old friend. He spoke English to everyone else, but insisted on speaking French with me because my limited French amused him. One time I tried to tell him that my cousin was coming to visit and that she could speak French fluently. But I couldn't remember the French word for cousin.

"My mother had a sister," I started out.

"Oh, your mother had a sister," he repeated with surprise.

"My mother had a sister and her sister had a daughter," I went on.

"Your mother had a sister... wait! My wife must hear this," and he went off to fetch his wife.

"Encore! You must listed carefully, my dear."

"My mother had a sister..."

"Her mother had a sister..."

"And her sister had a daughter..."

"Listen well, my dear, her mother had a sister and her sister had a daughter."

We had our laughs and when my cousin arrived she spoke fluent French and made all clear.

While we waited at the French customs, along came the old Mullah (the Muslim priest) of Ganta, who looked like one of the Hebrew patriarchs of Abraham's time. I had delivered three of the women of his household in difficult labor, two quite recently, and had had long discussions with him, through interpreters, on the advisability of educating the girls of the Mandingo tribe so as to create enlightened mothers. He greeted me most cordially and when I gave him a note to take back to Ganta mission he put it into his headdress and went off with a broad smile. After him came a young woman I knew from Monrovia, who spoke English and traveled up and down the country as a trader. She would have liked to join us in the Jeep, as she was going the same way, but had to stay with her cargo in the truck. She sent me a jar of guava jelly of her own making soon afterwards.

At last the trucks rolled toward Liberia and we got moving along the soft dirt main road to Zor Zor that had grass growing in the center. Most of the way it led through high bush that had not for generations been cut for farming. Low bush is woods, but high bush is glorious deep jungle.

Mid afternoon we came to Koule, and a river where the car ferry was not operating. There the Jeep turned back and the Zor Zor Jeep waited on the far side. There were two ways to cross the river, one a small ferry on empty oil drums, the other by native suspension bridge, built by weaving vines together to make a long V-shaped hammock reaching all the way across the river and suspended by vine-cables from many branches of trees on both sides. Such bridges were built by the men of the Poro Society, the big secret society headed by The Big Devil. Non-society people, including all women (except for one woman who held a position in the Poro), had to stay indoors and not even look out while the bridges were built. Such bridges were most cleverly constructed, and were used for years, with repairs as needed, but were fast being replaced by modern ones.

Naturally I wanted to cross by the vine bridge, but the mission servants who had come across the river to get me objected, "Good for us. Not good for you!" I took the ferry as they wished, but on the other side climbed up the high, ladder-like approach intending to go out on it. Then the reason for objection was clear. With bare feet people could walk in the V of the bridge sure-footed, but under my shoes the vines were exceedingly slippery. And I didn't want to go barefooted because of the jiggers on the vines, particularly unpleasant insects which bored into toes and made plenty of trouble. So with regret I climbed into the Jeep for the last part of the trip.

One of the Zor Zor teachers had driven to meet me, and it was well she was a good driver, for the road was narrow and rough, through very high bush, around plenty of sharp turns and down and up steep hills. But it was the most beautiful part of the trip, the trees so high and the light so subdued that there was little undergrowth. Late sunshine came through openings in bright, slanting beams, between the big tree trunks and masses of hanging vines. At one such place we stopped to eat supper before it grew dark. There was distant thunder, but the threatening storm held off as we crossed the border once more into Liberia and drove on to Zor Zor on a dry road.

The Lutheran hospital at Zor Zor was a lot further along than ours, with wards full of patients, a real operating room with enough space to get about in, real equipment and an x-ray outfit. Dr. Yung had made an x-ray table a couple of days before I arrived, and had done some good films. He was doing major surgery three days a week, with clinic on alternate days. They had three missionary nurses, and a training school that had been going long enough for them to have some trained local people to share responsibility. It gave me hope for what we might develop at Ganta. As it was, every time I did even minor surgery I crippled the clinic, where every last person who knew anything at all was needed.

The Zor Zor mission, like ours, was out from the town, but open enough for a view of the hills round about. Besides the hospital, they had a school and a workshop as we did, and an airfield on a nearby hill. The Lutheran mission also had a system of amateur radio operators, and somebody at each station took part every morning in an inter-station conversation, with somebody at Monrovia acting as chairman. At our mission it was often weeks between times when word came to us from Monrovia, and the furthest station at Barclayville seemed to be in altogether another world.

The Yung's fine little boy was born without incident, and I was soon on my way back to Ganta. It was a dry day, so at the river we sent my suitcase and typewriter across on the little raft, and I walked over the suspension bridge. It was not scary, but gave a delightful sensation of walking on air. The bridge developed a lovely swinging rhythm, up and down as well as laterally, owing to the elasticity of the vines and branches from which it hung. The approaches at both ends were like wide ladders, rather high to allow for the sag of the bridge and keep it above high-water level. When I asked the boy why he wouldn't let me walk over it the first time, he said, "If she had gotten hurt, the palaver would have been on my head!" And he was right, for that day it had been slippery.

Hills seem to be desirable places to missionaries. In Liberia, when we got a few days to rest, we went to a place called Mt. Bili where there was a very comfortable shack strongly built of rocks so that the animals wouldn't pull it apart. Mt. Bili was inland from Ganta, up a long trail through high bush with occasional giant kapok and mahogany trees with ferns, orchids and vines in their branches. The mountain was sacred, and at the foot of its high precipice many generations had made an annual sacrifice (only chickens in our day) to the spirits of the "old, old people," to assure plentiful harvests and happiness.

When the Harleys were building the little stone house at the top of Bili, Ya Zu, the survivor of former guardians of the mountain, who lived in the village at its foot, was distressed about the heavy rains hindering the work. The log of the place read, "He stood up one evening just after dark, and in a loud voice he called upon his ancestors by name. He apologized to them for the fact that we strangers had caught frogs in the stream and tumbled stones down the steep places. He asked forgiveness for these offenses, since the white people did not know any better, and implored them not to send any more storms. He said the white men had helped the black people in many ways. 'Before the white men came, we were like animals. They brought us iron. They brought us cloth. Now this white man has come to build a house on this mountain. Let him see good luck. Let the house catch the ground and become like part of the mountain itself!' "

Many times during the nights when we were in the stone house, there would come a loud banging on our door. We would rush to open it and find no one there. I soon learned it was the chimpanzees, who enjoyed the noise and perhaps liked to hear us rush to open the door.

The second time I went up I invited a new missionary to come with me. As we climbed the trail up the mountain I commented that we'd have a fine time doing watercolors. She laughed and said, "You'll have a fine time. I can't paint." But I said I had paints and brushes and enough for both of us, and "You'll try, surely?"

She was doubtful, but when we got settled I got out the paints and gave her some, and some papers on a board, and she took one site and I another, and she said, "What do I do?" So I showed her how to get her brush into action and went back to the doorway of the cottage to start my picture. It wasn't long until she began to say, "Oh, yes, here it is. Why here's that mountain on my paper." And she was quite amazed. After awhile she said, "Hyla, this is great fun, and it really looks like the scene I am looking at. This is my magnum opus. I shall keep it all my life."

While we were painting, Ya Zu and one of his sons brought us some fish. Ya Zu walked over to watch her painting, then said, "Why, there's that tree! And here's that tree! And there's that mountain! And here's my village down below! Oh, will you give that to me?"

And she said, "I'd be delighted to give that to you."

Ya Zu's son was learning English and was glad of a chance to use some of it. He told us about the Catholic mission where he went to school, then said, "I have learned a song. May I sing it for you?" So there he stood on top of the mountain looking out over miles and miles of unbroken jungle and sang a beautiful song in his own language. I asked him what it meant, and he said, "His word will stand. His word will stand, forever."

When Ya Zu and his son had gone, I said, "I thought that was your magnum opus and you were going to keep it all your life."

She answered, "Hyla, I'm so amazed I can put a scene on paper and have someone recognize it. I'm glad to give it to him and I'll make another for myself."

One December we had a picnic out at The Big Tree. We drove about three miles along the main road and just beyond the village of Dinamu, turned into a road Dr. Harley had built for hauling logs out of the bush. A couple of miles along that and we went through Wanao, a village that always intrigued me, tucked away as it was in the high bush far from anything else. A mile or so beyond that village we stopped in truly high bush: deep woods with high trees. Long vines with large leaves hanging down over our heads were orchids from which vanilla beans were gathered. Great ferns and aeroids grew on trunks and branches, and some vines were so strong we could swing from them.

The Big Tree was an enormous brown mahogany that stood out like a huge pillar of some giant cathedral, tall and straight, with buttress roots and sprawling roots out beyond those that were so big we could sit on them.

At the base of that majestic tree we saw a most beautiful and fragile dance of insects like mosquito hawks, but much lighter and slimmer, with legs like thin cobwebs. A huge layer of these insects clung to the tree roots. Each held two feet up to another layer of insects which grasped them and lifted two feet of their own to another layer above, and so on, layer after layer, all with wings aquiver in a network all but invisible, like a cloud of thin smoke waving rhythmically back and forth, apparently for the sheer joy of motion. All but the first layer were flying continuously in a most intricate formation flying.

Ever since hearing of Gipo, the town of the "bravest people in the country," the town of the man who was bitten by a snake while up in a palm tree, I had wanted to go there to see it. It wasn't a long trip. Our Jeep took us and three Mano boys along the big road to Dinamu, where we turned off the motor road to follow one of Dr. Harley's logging roads. Three miles in we came to Wanau where we had watched the witch-hunt in session, and on from Wanau through beautiful high bush past the place where Winifred Harley had found a previously unknown fern, on up to The Big Tree. We looked for the curious dancing insects, the *yidi nga-nga-nga,* as we had learned they were called, and there they were down between the great buttress roots, doing their strange and beautiful dance.

A mile or so beyond The Big Tree the road became impassable for our Jeep, so we pushed on by foot through the silent green beauty of the high bush. There was a wealth of ferns and vines and aeroids, trees like banyans with a network of branches and high buttress roots, others that apparently danced lightly on their root tips, their roots well above ground with plenty of room for wild creatures underneath. Ahead on the trail shone a bright spot: a small red Coca Cola cooler that our steward proudly carried on his head to bring back eggs that we hoped to buy at Gipo.

The whole walk was only about an hour, and we stopped for lunch near the town at Gipo Waterside, where the women of the town were doing the wash. We crossed the stream by walking a fallen tree, passed a great bombax that was long the recipient of sacrifice, and were soon in Gipo. Johnny Gipo, one of its leading citizens, had invited us to be his guests. He came hurrying to meet us and to welcome us to his clean and neat, rectangular house that had large screened windows.

There the town people came to greet us with their exquisite grace and courtesy. We bought some eggs and fine big pineapples, and Johnny Gipo presented us with some rice, okra and eggs from his farm. We shared a tin of hamburgers and some chocolate bars, and a British *Illustrated Post*. Then a woman we had treated at the clinic years before came with a gift of two eggs, and another former patient sent for us for medical advice.

The town had gotten its reputation as that of the bravest people in the country because they had had the most powerful arrow poison. It was greatly feared, with reason, by the government troops during the wars of a generation or two earlier. But in a walk about the town they seemed to have become most peaceful. We saw two blacksmith shops under thatch roofs. In each the smith sat on the ground pounding the edge of a cutlass blade to thin it out, using an iron hammer with a bent wooden handle like a dried deer leg. Each shop had its bellows, two separate leather bags connected by a Y tube to the blow-tube, but the cutlass blades were being pounded cold. We visited their new mud-and-thatch church, and saw a ballfield in process of construction. From Gipo to Flumpa was only a couple of miles, and the young people of Flumpa had learned to play soccer at the Irish mission there.

We saw two wooden drums, one standing higher than my head and two to three feet across, that once called the brave Gipo men to war. In recent years the drums had been used only for music when the people danced. We asked the Gipo people whether they really were the bravest people in the country. They laughed and said, "Of course!" When we mentioned their famous arrow poison, they said, "It is so strong that if we shoot an arrow with that poison into a green tree, the tree will die!"

In front of one house we saw five women sitting in a row on the ground, each one being scrubbed by somebody else, with a crowd of women standing about. All five had their hair combed out of the usual braids, standing out straight. After the scrubbing an old woman walked along the row and poured water out of a calabash on each woman's head. The five were widows of a man who had died the year before, and this was their ceremonial cleansing. Afterwards they put on new clothes and beads, had a grand feast and were then ready to marry somebody else.

A crowd of small children followed us about the town, and when we started for home escorted us down to the waterside, ran out on the fallen-tree bridge and leaped down into the stream. They splashed about with great shouting and jumping, wet dark skin shining in the sun like polished metal, full of the same joy of life that fills children in swimming holes the world over.

George and Winifred Harley with a government visitor. With the improved road from Monrovia came many visitors: Lady Dorothy Mills (*Through Liberia*. London: 1926); Graham Greene with his cousin Barbara (*Journey Without Maps*. New York: Double-day, 1936). "There were people with an interest in anthropology," wrote Winifred, "or architecture; politics or public health; and others who wanted to talk about butterflies, flowers or snails. A New York Port Authority consultant drove up with his wife, who turned out to be a former Trinity classmate. President Tubman sent Galbraith Welch (*The Jet Lighthouse*. London: Museum Press, 1960). We welcomed a millionaire couple looking forward to establishing their own medical mission; twenty-five...Methodists from the U.S.A.; diplomats; Bishops and Board secretaries. There were travelers from almost every part of the world; an Israeli promoter gave us a bottle of Jordan River water, a Russian guest left an inkwell in the form of the 'King of Bells' in the Kremlin. There was an Italian trader, a traveler from south India, a member of the British House of Commons, a Chinese businessman and many others."

Photo courtesy of Eugene L. Harley

George and Winifred Harley at the dedication of the new chapel, 1949. This was the last building constructed under Dr. Harley's direction. The Harleys retired in 1960.

Photo courtesy of Eugene L. Harley

Paying our Debt to Africa

All the time that I was in Ganta the mission was in a period of expansion, Dr. Harley's determination to try to keep pace, in our small corner, with the rapid development in Liberia. It was a part of Africa's awakening and her resolution no longer to be referred to as the Dark Continent. As missionaries we felt that we owed a tremendous debt to Africa, not only because of past exploitation, but for her immense riches in iron, gold, copper, uranium, rubber and cocoa. That debt to Africa we could never pay in full, but we could pay the interest on it by our services to the sick and poor. We could make small payments on the principal by educating and training the Africans to take over as fast as possible Africa's full share of her own development.*

The kind of help being poured into African countries by Point Four, World Health, and other agencies was far from enough. Although they had borrowed ideas and plans that missionaries had been using for generations, too often they lacked the brotherly love that made philanthropy and technical advice palatable to the proud.

Dr. Harley believed that our missions supplied that lacking ingredient, and he had big plans for Ganta. Our industrial work made a favorable impression on visitors. They liked to go out to the log road and see the big forest trees. They liked to watch the sawmill run, and were interested in what the schoolboys made in the carpenter shop. The chances were that each visitor would need

---

* "All missionaries [by 1960] had heard the warning: 'In view of the political upheavals in the world, and the urge toward nationalism... Prepare future leaders in your country *now* to take over your responsibilities; lest when the time for change arrives you have no one trained and ready.' Stepping aside is a hard thing to do; but at Ganta we were working toward that end."   — *Winifred J. Harley*

repairs to his car after 180 miles of dirt road from Monrovia. Our garage mechanics could make some repairs that could not be done on the coast. Sometimes Dr. Harley made new parts in the blacksmith shop or on the lathe. But we needed to move the blacksmithy and the lathe out of the tiny engine room where, if a schoolboy wanted to learn how to do it he had to watch Dr. Harley through the window. We needed a small building for machine-shop activities. We needed a new anvil. We needed wood-working tools for the school furniture shop. Deterioration is a real problem in the tropics.

Our Industrial Department was developed to furnish us with materials for buildings and furniture needed on the Mission. But of equal importance was its function to train schoolboys and apprentices. We employed about one hundred men of varying skills: mechanics, blacksmiths, carpenters, brick masons, stone masons, lumber men, brick and tile makers, and a truck driver. All had learned their skills at Ganta Mission.

Our 1947 Ford pickup truck was rebuilt twice, once when it ran into a tree, another time when a tree fell on it. We had grown so rapidly that we needed a Jeep for the evangelistic missionary and another for the medical household, to serve also as an ambulance. Electric light and plumbing were installed in our dwellings and the small hospital. The brick yard was largely mechanized, but clay was still being pulverized by hand for thousands of roofing tiles.

We needed our house on Mt. Bili, but for some the 3,400-foot climb was too strenuous. Dr. Harley cut a new trail, the lower part widened into a road that would let cars go partway up. We needed to build a halfway house, where those who couldn't do much climbing could enjoy at least some change of climate and pace of life.

We had erected a stone church in the Mission clearing, but before it was completed realized it should be made larger. We had a good school, 125 boys in dormitories and thirty girls living in the villages. We set aside twenty-five acres to use for a girls' campus and needed to build them a dormitory. We had blackboards of a sort, but needed better ones. We had a little secondhand electric plant for the school compound, but needed a generator to more adequately fill the need. We had eight grades at Ganta school, but it was the conviction of missionaries all over Africa that the burden of educating still rested so heavily on the missions that our slogan should be, "Add a grade every two years." We needed more teachers, and we needed to pay them better.

We had a mission staff, aided by three young Liberians, who held twenty religious services each week. But other friendly nearby villages also wanted churches and their own pastor in place of a missionary coming only once a week. We needed equipment for those village churches, and men educated beyond that of the young exhorters who had had but an eighth grade education.

Our medical work was almost self-supporting from fees brought in by patients. But it was largely an outpatient clinic. We opened one ward with twenty-five beds, but the nearest real hospital was one hundred miles away. Plans for two more wards were approved, and a wing for kitchen/dining room/laundry, and another for the operating room.

The Women's Division of the Methodist Church sent staff to Ganta, increasing our medical personnel almost one hundred percent. We needed residences for their nurses and student nurses. The two missionary nurses could not do all the nursing. We needed Liberian girls to help, and they had to be trained. By the time I retired in 1961, a great deal of progress had been made toward all these goals, and there had been many changes among our missionary staff.

To look ahead to what was still needed was important, but to look backward gave hope for the future. When George and Winifred Harley retired in 1960, Winifred noted that they left the abandoned rice field they found in 1926 "a beautifully landscaped campus with some twenty-five good buildings of stone, wood, brick, and cement." They also left behind a well of goodwill and many African friends in better health who were better educated and skilled in crafts and professions than they would have been without Ganta Mission. These have made important contributions to their own and other nations.

On to Tombouctou—and Tupper Lake

In 1959 I reached the Board's retirement age of sixty-five in the middle of a term, and by the grace of God they allowed me to stay on for two extra years. But they refused my request to be reassigned to Ganta for another term. The idea of sailing from the west coast of Africa straight across the Atlantic to return to Tupper Lake didn't appeal to me, so I asked Mildred Black, who was as crazy as I was, to go across Africa with me.

Before we set out, the Muslim leaders prayed all night for our safe journey. Roy Watkins, a Baptist missionary, did all sorts of errands around Liberia by air, and as arranged, he set down his Piper Cub on the main road to pick us up for the first leg of our journey to the Cavally River. We set off with lots of beautiful farewell speeches ringing in our ears and sorrow in our hearts to be leaving good friends. Mildred and I sat diagonally on a board placed across the armrest of the one passenger seat where there was nothing to break our view forward or to each side as we covered in a few hours what took days to travel on foot, looking down on beautiful high bush with each tree set off by its own shadow.

We had thought to cross the Cavally by dugout, but the river was low with many rocks and a swift current, and we were talked into accepting piggyback rides from men who were accustomed to giving them. Hauling myself up the steep bank of the Cavally River, on a network of vines and roots, into the Ivory Coast, I suddenly realized I was actually on my way to Tombouctou, Cairo and Jerusalem, names that had enchanted me from childhood.

After scrambling up the far bank, we had a long walk along a bush trail with four baggage carriers toting on their heads our one suitcase each, food, blankets and water filter. It was a lovely, shady walk past some of the biggest trees I've ever seen, with lots of vines and ferns and singing birds. Suddenly we saw the carriers stop, lay down their loads and pick up stones; we hurried to catch up with them to see what wild animal threatened. If it had been a python or leopard, they would have known what to do, but it was cows. They had never seen a cow before because there were none left in Liberia where tsetse flies killed them with sleeping sickness. We earned a reputation for great valor as we led them past the cows.

After half an hour we came to a motor road where a tall local gentleman greeted us genially in French. Hung around his neck was an impressive medicine made of cowrie shells and leopard's teeth. No car was in sight, so we started walking in the direction of Toulepleu. Two and a half hours later we came to a chain across the road, and there on a shaded bamboo bench where our road met the main road, we had lunch with an audience of local people and waited for a car to come along. After a while a man suggested that to get a car it would be useful to write a letter in French, so with the help of a dictionary we set to work. The local people selected a messenger, I pulled out money for him, and then they wanted to know where to carry the letter. We said we didn't know, didn't they? No, they didn't, so I put money and letter back in my bag.

Finally we walked along the main road to a village, and there under the shade of a huge mango tree the villagers set two impressive chairs for us, then lined up and gazed at us until a bus came along. That bus. We sailed over hills, around corners, through puddles, and through a hole in the floor every puddle sent up a generous fountain of mud.

The driver stopped beside a small shop where he ordered a bottle of beer, took a long swig himself and passed it around to his passengers. He was amazed that we preferred water from a plastic bottle we carried. With a small hand-pump filter we had no problem getting dependable drinking water. From time to time we were also able to buy cold carbonated "limonade" or "orange croosh."

At Toulepleu the driver led us to the Ivory Coast customs where the *Douanier,* lying in a deck chair under a tree greeted us graciously, made sure we carried no revolvers and waved us on to the commandant to get our passports stamped. A huge crowd surrounded the commandant's office, and when we finally got inside a completely naked man ran straight at us, and behind him, two more. Within a couple of feet of us they turned and ran the other direction. The commandant charmingly explained that the men were getting heart-stress tests before induction into the army.

We stayed overnight at the *campment,* a clean, comfortable government rest house where we could heat some dehydrated soup for supper, and in the morning the owner of the *rapide* (truck) got us to Man, a large town surrounded by mountains, where he located a *rapide* bound for Beoumi, another eight-hour ride including a ferry ride across the Sassandro River where a barge hitched to a cable and pushed by the current got us across.

At Beoumi we stayed overnight with a mission family and I was called on to help a man in great pain who wanted his tooth extracted. I had forceps with me, but no Novocain, and I don't know how he stood it, but the tooth finally came out. There appear to be three rules about pulling a tooth: you make sure you get the right one, get a good grip on it, and never let go.

Next morning, as we were discussing transportation to Bouake, in drove two missionaries bound for that town who agreed to take us along. At Bouake we spent the weekend resting, writing, getting our yellow fever and smallpox vaccinations and our tickets to Bobo Dioulasso. We had never been on a train in Africa before, and were excited to be finally heading north toward Tombouctou. The train wasn't crowded, our seats were comfortable for the nine-hour trip to Upper Volta, and at each station people brought pans of delicious mangoes that we munched as we looked out at the barren countryside of dry grass and scraggly bushes. The house roofs gradually became less steep as we headed toward the Sahara Desert, and finally at Bobo Dioulasso many of the mud roofs were absolutely flat.

We were thankful it had been smooth sailing so far, and stayed at a mission guest house for a couple of days where we had quiet, restful nights occasionally interrupted by the boom of a heavy mango falling on the corrugated zinc roof, then rolling down and hitting the ground. Bats chewed the mangoes, leaving the seed hanging on the stem, and after a certain amount of chewing, down went the rest of the fruit. The bats followed them down and ate the rest on the ground. We enjoyed Bobo Dioulasso, especially its colorful big market where one bought anything from dried tomato powder and onions to motorcycles, and gorgeous flame trees shaded us all.

Our truck for Mopti was to leave at three one afternoon, so we arrived early. Three trucks were lined up to make the trip and we were told to pick out which one we wanted to ride in. One had *Dieu Merci* painted on it, which appealed to us, but we were told its rearview mirror was no good. Someone said the tires on the other two were not so good and a rearview mirror wasn't much use because there was so much dust you couldn't see anything in it. So we boarded *Dieu Merci.*

The other two trucks soon left, but our driver showed up two hours later, and we took off only to run into a traffic inspector who disliked our rearview mirror, took away the truck papers and told the driver to return to town to pay a fine to get them back.

After eight we finally got started, and the driver tried to cheer us by buying us each a big bottle of *yougi,* the local soft drink, but soon we were stopped again by something going wrong under the hood. The driver tinkered and cranked and off we went, but this happened once an hour thereafter. Near midnight we reached Mali where we had to open our luggage for Upper Volta inspectors. About four in the morning we detoured to Sann to let off a passenger, and everyone clamored for a stop to sleep. We were given two hours, found a very dirty *campment,* but thankfully stretched out.

At six we were in our appointed places on the *Dieu Merci,* where we sat for an hour and a half as new passengers were signed on. The heat was intense, not unbearable except when we stopped, which was frequently. At one underhood ailment stop we noticed that the radiator was boiling over, but that no notice was taken of it. We mentioned it to the driver, but he wasn't alarmed. Inevitably the engine ceased to function in the middle of nowhere, with no shade and our water nearly gone. The biscuits we had with us were too dry to go down without water, and we hadn't eaten since lunch the day before.

We suggested we might transfer to some passing vehicle, but the driver was not enthusiastic and kept saying we would start immediately. Finally, mid afternoon, Mildred flagged down a passing gas truck. The driver obligingly strapped our loads to the spare tire, and about five in the afternoon we reached Mopti, bushed, having had too little water, food and sleep, and too much sun for more than a day. At Mopti we found a closed mission where a kind watchman and his wife turned up after a while and made us a charcoal fire to heat water for some of our dehydrated soup, and helped us put up mosquito nets over a bed in the yard. Next day we moved over to a government *campment* where there was plenty of water and good French food.

Mopti was a fish town on the Niger River, and we stayed there several days. We had hoped to take a barge to Tombouctou, but after our experience of too much sun we lost our enthusiasm for haphazard travel and were relieved to find the barges all aground because of low water. So we went to Air France, where we sat and watched the populace while we waited for a plane. Men were in long gowns, often made of goat or camel hair country cloth, and strange trousers built like enormous pillowcases with foot holes at the lower corners. Women were in gaily-colored dresses, each with a short skirt over a long one, with a voluminous and diaphanous long gown enveloping all the rest, and gay headcloths in many becoming shapes. Men's headgear ranged from turbans of many shapes, some enveloping the face as well as the head, to red fezzes and umbrella-like sunhats up to nearly a yard wide, with a fancy center handle on top. Women's earrings were a study in themselves. Frequently each ear sported ten or a dozen gold rings. Some heavy gold rings hung from a hole in the earlobe, part of their weight carried by a strand of yarn over the top of the ear. Some women wore gold nose rings as well.

After a dither when the plane arrived, when at first no Mopti passengers were to be allowed to board, the difficulty was ironed out and we took off in a fine air-conditioned plane with cold apple juice served to all hands.

At Tombouctou there was a landing strip but no airport, and no agency in the town. While we stood under the plane in the shade waiting for our luggage, the French pilot answered our question about how we would get a plane to go on to Gao. There was no schedule, he said, but a plane might come along in a few days or a couple of weeks, and passengers just went out and got on board when the *campment* manager sensed the plane was to arrive.

But there we actually were in Tombouctou, standing under the wing of a plane at high noon, surrounded by a lot of men in long gowns and turbans. A Landrover took us all off through scrubby thorn trees to the town and the nicest *campment* yet, with a beautiful terrace that had a fountain in the middle and mosaics around it. Flowers surrounded the terrace and bordered wide steps that led down to the lake shore below.

What a wonderful week we had, exploring the city and visiting with new friends, sleeping out on the terrace where it was heavenly and balmy. Sometimes in the night, in the bright moonlight, there was a lot of splashing and grunting below our terrace. The first night we didn't know what the noise was and got up to see. Silhouetted against the sky, just starting to brighten, was a long line of camels loaded with blocks of salt. They filed in over the horizon toward us and when they reached the lake below they and their masters all got into the water together.

Among our new friends were two French gentlemen who stayed at the *campment* while working on what would be an airport. They said the temperature often reached 62 degrees C, which translated to about 144 degrees F. We were surprised, so they invited us to come to their place at 11:30 next morning to read their thermometer. We thought it was a cool day, but the thermometer read 50 degrees C, which was 122 degrees F.

Sand kept blowing in from the desert, piling up against walls and steadily raising the level of the city so that what were apparently low walls and buildings were sometimes the tops of buried ones. We wondered if there were a special trick to walking on sand, and whether snowshoes might help. We browsed through the market, visited a fortress and mosque and a Koranic school, watched women baking bread in huge beehive mud ovens, and a woman making belts and baskets of gay beadwork, using modern dress snappers for fastenings, as she sat in the sand of her shop floor. We watched trains of donkeys and camels loaded with slabs of rock salt come in from the desert, had rides on a camel, and at the invitation of a policeman wound up at headquarters for a routine check of foreigners. In a carpenter shop craftsmen proudly showed us doors and windows, cupboards and doorposts they were making, and let us try their drill. It was turned by ropes that twisted the upright center rapidly back and forth as one moved a crossbar up and down, with ropes that wound up and slacked around the upright. It looked easy, but it took several tries before I could work it.

When the day came that the *campment* manager felt a plane was about to arrive, we caught the plane to Gao, where we got a Trans-African bus to Dogondoutchi in Niger. Across from us on the bus sat a kindly Haji. Having been to Mecca, he approved of our journey to Jerusalem. He told us that the many horizontal beams projecting from mosque towers were to encourage storks to nest there; just as in Strassburg, storks were considered a good omen.

At six o'clock our driver pulled off the road and everybody got out and prayed. We did, too, but not kneeling with foreheads in the sand as our Muslim neighbors did. We had an unexpectedly comfortable night at the Ayerou *campment,* which we reached about midnight. The Haji walked with us to be sure we found it, then went off to sleep elsewhere himself. He appeared next morning to make sure we got to the bus on time, and we shared our date-cake breakfast with him. He told us to watch for giraffes, and sure enough, they were close by the road, mottled in beautiful tan, with strong necks like towers and heads higher than the treetops.

At Yantella we had a rest and got visas for the Sudan, and at Dogondoutchi changed busses for Birni'n Koni. That bus was so packed that Mildred sat practically in the laps of two gentlemen to the voluble indignation of one wife. We arrived late at night at Biri'n Koni, made our way to the *campment* where the plumbing would have been better if it had not existed, and slept in the dining room with an African woman and four men.

At Maradi we stayed in a mission gatehouse over the weekend, and a Piper Comanche of the Sudan Interior Mission took us along to Kano, Nigeria, where we made arrangements to fly over the desert to Khartoum. There was only one plane a week to Khartoum, so we made sure not to miss it, and enjoyed a relaxed, smooth flight with a glorious sunrise and arrived about five in the morning with barely time to get through the various airport ceremonies and make the train for Wadi Halfi and our boat down the rest of the Nile.

Our ship down the Nile turned out to be a flotilla of four boats fastened together with the engine in the central boat that had a stern paddle wheel and propelled all four boats. Our cabin was in a boat to one side, a third was on the other side and the fourth was pushed ahead. We used public baths and had been told to get a bath as soon as we boarded because there was always such a rush for the bathrooms. So we got early baths and went to bed. When almost asleep somebody put his head through our window, turned on the light, said, "Flit," and sprayed the whole room. We went back to sleep and near midnight were wakened by shouts of "Abu Simbel." It dawned on Mildred that it was probably the location of the ancient temple soon to be flooded by the Aswan Dam, so we grabbed housecoats and flashlight and went down the gangplank into the night. My rubber bath shoes kept coming off in the sand, so I took them off altogether to explore that dark, mysterious temple full of carved figures, columns, hieroglyphics, wall paintings, and a painting of huge sweeping wings across the ceiling. We realized how great was Egyptian history, mythology and symbolism, and resolved to learn something about it.

It was good to be on a ship again, and at El Shallal we were treated to a most amazing demonstration of expert handling of our awkward group of four ships lashed together. With the aid of a searchlight in the bow that night, our pilot maneuvered the lot into a narrow space between high, rocky banks, and between other rocks reaching up from depths nearly to the surface. It was hair-raising, but so cleverly done without jar or bump that all four boats missed by inches rocks to starboard, then swung across and came gently to rest against equally formidable rocks to port, where men sprang ashore with ropes and made fast.

We took a local train down to Luxor, with never a dull moment. First an Egyptian man of some education struck up conversation, proposed marriage to each of us and was not in the least abashed at being repeatedly turned down. Our rejected but smiling suitor got off at his station with smiles and handshakes, then ran back with two stalks of sugarcane as a parting gift.

Next were several more men, friendly but more reserved. As the most conversationally inclined was about to leave, he called out the window to a small boy to cut him some sugarcane stalks from a standing freight train. With a smile and a bow he handed us half a dozen stalks and bowed out. What is the courteous and ethical procedure when presented with stolen sugarcane by a gracious person with whom conversation is limited to a few words and sign language? We shared the sugarcane with two families who were next to fill our compartment. They had a newspaper, so presently we were making Jacob's Ladders and they showed us how to make airplanes and a figure that waved both arms like semaphores. Our last neighbor was Mr. Abul, a dignified gentleman in a black beret who, when he found we had no Egyptian coins for porters, carried our suitcases all the way to the street and got us into a Victoria.

Mr. Abul, who had been guiding tourists to Karnak for forty-two years, took us there next day, entering between two rows of "Sbhinkuses with rams' heads." Arabic has no "p" sound and we rather enjoyed his charming explanations as we began our education in Egyptian antiquities: the ways of ancient "nobils" who "brayed under a roof," and the "boor beebil" who "brayed in an open court;" of statues and columns of the earthquake of 23 B.C. which "shoom down," and of the "boorfacer" who dug in the rubbish and "read the cartouches and saw which and which, and buildum ub again."

Mr. Abul told us of the ambitions and jealousies and teachings and cruelties of the ancients, of their many efforts to placate the various gods and to assure their future life; of their tremendous works to assure everlasting fame. He showed it all to us in the designs that "the engineers signed in stone"...the misery of thousands of slaves, the pettiness of the powerful, the present-day avarice of "the beebil. They came by night and cuddit out and sold it to the tourists."

Karnak. Luxor. Thebes. The Colossi of Memnon. The Valley of the Nobles, Valley of the Kings and of course the tomb of young Tutankhamen. We did it all.

It was nearly the end of May. We had a dusty hot trip up the Nile to visit friends in the United Presbyterian Mission and a ride on their lovely two-masted ship, the *Ibis*. More than a hundred years earlier an Indian prince had called at this mission and requested the head of its girls' school to pick out for him a wife who could read and write. One of the girls was chosen and the prospect put to her and her family, who were delighted with the idea of her becoming queen of an Indian state. So she and the prince were married and the prince built the *Ibis* to take them on their honeymoon. When they went to India the prince, much pleased with his new wife, presented the *Ibis* to the mission. They needed a boat large enough to live on for their trips up and down the Nile, and more than a hundred years later the *Ibis* was still in use, just because a girl who could read and write was willing to marry an Indian prince.

Mildred came down with fever that worsened, and she obviously needed to be in hospital, so we flew to Cairo. I did all sorts of business and took the tours while she was laid up. Finally she recovered and we returned to some of the places I had explored, then took off for Israel. This was before the Six Day War, which gave all of Jerusalem to Israel. We were not allowed to have an Israeli visa, but had a separate document from an Israeli ambassador which would admit us to Israel. From Egypt we flew to the Jordan part of Jerusalem and stayed there for about a week. Then we hired a taxi which took us near the Mandelbaum Gate. There we climbed out of the taxi and walked into Israel.

For so long we had been saying, "My feet shall stand within thy gates, O Jerusalem," and there we were. For the next two weeks we did it all in Israel, and left with great regret. The experience that meant the most to me was one afternoon when I joined the weekly procession along the Via Dolorosa with about a dozen Franciscans. We carried a full-sized wooden cross. It was heavy. Several of us would carry it to one station, where we would set it down and listen to the Franciscan leader say, "Here, in this very place..." then another group would carry the cross to the next station.

June 22 was a shining day for sailing, and the *M.V. Tappuz* was a pleasant Israeli freighter that carried seven passengers. The ship was riding high when we boarded at Haifa, drawing only eleven feet, but she was loading great cubic blocks of marble and bundles of plywood.

We sailed around through the Straits of Messina, past Aetna and Stromboli, with a stop at Naples and a sail up the coast to Livorno; then Genoa, Gibraltar, Lisbon, nine days across the Atlantic to The St. Lawrence Seaway and Montreal. Toward the end of July, three months after leaving Ganta, I was home in Tupper Lake.

Hyla Doc and Mildred Black about to take off in the Piper Cub for points north and east across Africa in 1961. Runway was the main road that passed through Ganta Mission to the coast. *Photo courtesy of Mildred A. Black.*

Hyla Doc crossing the Cavally River
Photo by Mildred A. Black

"Hauling myself up the steep bank of the Cavally River, on a network of vines and roots, into the Ivory Coast, I suddenly realized I was actually on my way to Tombouctou, Cairo and Jerusalem, names that had enchanted me from childhood." Hyla Doc.

Photo by Mildred A. Black

Dieu Merci at Bobo Dioulasso

Photo by Mildred A. Black

Dieu Merci on road to Mopti

Photo by Mildred A. Black

Guest house at Tombouctou.

Photo by Mildred A. Black

This is how Tombouctou's ancient cities were buried under drifting sands.
Photo by Mildred A. Black

Donkey carrying hay at Tombouctou.
Photo by Mildred A. Black

Hyla Doc tries out the local transportation, Tombouctou.
Photo by Mildred A. Black

Transafricaine bus from Gao, Mali, to Naimey, Niger.
Photo by Mildred A. Black

Via Dolorosa, Jerusalem.

Photo by Mildred A. Black

Israeli cargo ship *M.V. Tappuz*, Haifa to Montreal.

Photo by Mildred A. Black

Dan Allen and Hyla Doc
sailing Dr. David A.
Johnson's boat on Tupper
Lake.
Photos by David A. Johnson

A New Burst of Energy

Charles R. Britt
Missionary Evangelist, Ganta, 1948-1950, 1952

The coming of Dr. Hyla Watters to Liberia was a great day for the nation, a high-water mark in the history of The Ganta United Methodist Mission. Dr. and Mrs. George Harley, assisted by Mildred Black, Ruth Longstaff, Martha and B.B. Cofield, had laid the mission's foundations. The arrivals of Hyla Watters and Dagmar Petersen, R.N., soon followed by Uniola Adams, R.N. and Margaret Prentice, R.N., who came to us from the China field, marked an urgently-needed step forward.

Hyla brought, in addition to her medical skills, her Christian commitment, her enthusiasm for learning to know the Mano and other tribespeople, her interest in everybody and everything. A new burst of energy swept across the program in all its facets.

Following Hyla's departure for "retirement" (which few who knew her ever believed would actually occur), the years were marked by rise and fall in the medical program. One of the great moments was when Dr. Wilfred Boayue, himself a Liberian, son of a great chief of the Mano people, inspired by Hyla to become a surgeon, assumed Medical Directorship. Other medical personnel through the years included eight physicians and a number of nurses, several from Scandinavia. Loretta Gruver, R.N., merits special mention: she served Ganta for more than twenty-five years and was among the first to return to Ganta when the 1992 cease-fire was agreed to during the civil war.

Through the years great progress was made toward training medical personnel, especially the nurses' training program under

Loretta Gruver's leadership. The Winifred Harley School of Nursing was, for a long time, one of three principal sources of trained medical personnel for the nation. Later the Liberian government opened a medical school in Monrovia.

The program for leprosy diagnosis, treatment and rehabilitation had been pioneered by the Harleys, Mildred Black, Ruth Longstaff and Dagmar Petersen. Uniola Adams did more for the leprosy program than anyone else. Among other contributions, she started the wood carving project so that the lepers could earn money. Hyla's arrival forwarded that program. It reached its peak under the leadership of Dr. Paul Getty, when it became an international training center for leprosy treatment. Today that work is primarily in the hands of an Irish Roman Catholic order of nuns.

The civil war has caused great suffering. There will be much need for rehabilitation once it is resolved and the people are allowed to return to their gentle pattern of life, to get on with the task of building a strong nation.

Charles Britt, first full-time evangelist at Ganta Mission, 1948.
Photo courtesy of Charles Britt

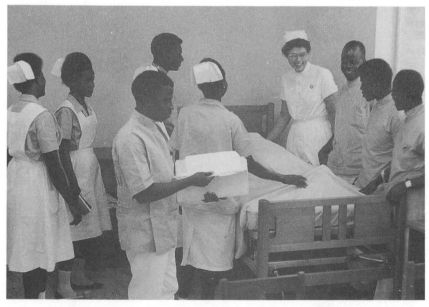

Loretta Gruver, R.N., served Ganta Mission for more than twenty-five years. She was the first to return to Ganta during the 1992 cease-fire.

Ruth Longstaff Burgess teaching Wuo Gahpay to write. Ruth, along with the Harleys, Mildred Black and Dagman Petersen, pioneered the leprosy program.

Photo by Mildred A. Black

Liberia, A Unique African Nation

Remarkable world events in recent years have overshadowed Liberia's bitter civil war; this small African republic, barely the size of Ohio, seldom catches world attention, as it did in October 1992 with the murder of five American nuns. There were mixed motives that led to this anomaly of a republic, settled by freed slaves from America, in the vast continent of Africa. Perhaps a brief sketch of Liberia's unique history is in order.

What to do about freed slaves in America was a baffling question long before 1776. Many settlers believed slavery to be wicked, and had freed several thousands. Many also were of a mind that any people, if thrown upon their own resources, could achieve and govern a free society. Three years before the Revolution a New England clergyman, Samuel Hopkins, devised a plan to train them to be colonizers and missionaries in Africa. Eight years later, in 1781, Thomas Jefferson outlined a plan coupling a gradual abolition of slavery with a subsidized settling of former slaves in Africa. By 1794 Congress began enacting a series of laws designed to end slave trade between American and foreign powers, but the "African Statues" were openly violated.

In 1817 American Colonization Societies appeared in cities along the East Coast. They were started by missionaries and semi-informally adopted by the state legislatures of Maryland and Virginia, which as early as 1800 had requested Congress to "...correspond with the President on the subject of purchasing land...whither persons obnoxious to the law or dangerous to the peace of society [freed slaves who might push for complete emancipation] may be removed."

In 1818 Congress defined slavery as piracy and instructed the U.S. Navy to seize any American slavers and to drop the slaves off along the Grain Coast. This southern coast of the West African bulge gained its name from the "Grain of Paradise," seed from the pipili or melequeta pepper, a species related to banana and ginger, which produced a much sought after spice. In 1819 President James Monroe approved purchase of a site along the West African coast, and its first settlement, Monrovia, was named for him. A mere fifteen hundred freed slaves first braved that fever-ridden coast.

These Americo-Liberians, from diverse African cultures, adopted the trappings of power they had seen in the Old South. They built replicas of southern mansions, wore high hats and long-tailed coats, carried canes, kept concubines, disdained manual labor. They were the elite. Filling the hinterland were more than a million indigenous people in more than twenty tribes, each with its own culture, language and territory.

Named from the word "liberty," Liberia, which in Latin means "free land," dates its founding by the American Colonization Society (by then a single entity) in 1822, although it did not become a republic until 1847. Great Britain created a crisis in 1845 by refusing to pay custom levies to a commercial enterprise which was not a sovereign state. The U.S. didn't want to declare Liberia a colony, and independence was the only solution. With Joseph Jenkins Roberts from Virginia as its first president, Liberia became the second independent nation of black citizens; only Haiti could claim to be older.

There continued to be a close relationship to the United States. Many acres of land were granted to the Firestone Company on a ninety-nine year lease to develop rubber plantations. During the Second World War Liberia quickly declared itself an ally, and the U.S. used Liberia as a base. A large airfield was built and the Monrovia harbor modernized so that ships could dock and not have to unload while riding at anchor. In 1948 American businessmen, in concert with the Liberian government, began to encourage cocoa-growing and the use of the country's magnificent timber resources. They also built a railroad to link iron mines in the north with the coast.

Throughout her first century Liberia was beset by tribal conflicts and by dependence on aid that encouraged foreign encroachment on her territory; Britain and France seized nearly half the original land area. It is something of a miracle that Liberia survived. Two outstanding presidents infused the nation with the spirit and courage to disentangle herself from colonial dependencies. Arthur Barclay, in his 1932 inaugural, pledged to establish law and order, to rehabilitate her international reputation, lay a base for economic independence, secure some financial freedom for the government and to initiate works of social benefit.

But the real turning point was in 1944 with the election of William Vacanarat Shadrack Tubman. Under his leadership Liberia became a model republic, making astonishing progress toward unification as a nation with an open door and pay-as-you-go policy. President Tubman, reelected five times, was a dynamic leader who also developed more economic and political opportunities for the indigenous people. It was within his terms as president (1944-1967) that Hyla Doc worked in Liberia.

Vice President William R. Tolbert succeeded to the presidency on Tubman's death and tried to follow Tubman's policies. But with a rise in the cost of rice, the nation's basic food, coupled with price drops in its major exports, iron ore and rubber, tensions between Americo-Liberians and the various tribes increased. They erupted in earnest in 1980, when a small group of indigenous military men killed Tolbert and installed Samuel K. Doe, an army sergeant, as president.

Doe's rule was brutal and corrupt. Throughout his government funds were diverted to private pockets. Doe killed anyone who opposed him; among those detained and jailed, some flogged for "anti-government activities," were Western journalists. U.S. Marines airlifted seventy-four Americans to safety.

John Butin, at the Carter Center at Emory University in Atlanta, has drawn up a closely detailed account of the current conflict. In short, the Reagan administration strongly supported the Doe government between 1980 and 1985, and extended $400 million in aid (the largest amount of aid per capita the U.S. offered any African state) to the country for "modernizing the troops" and guaranteeing elections in 1985.

Doe administration's abuses, corruption and mismanagement prompted several attempts to overthrow him. In 1981 Doe executed five of his former close associates for their part in a failed coup. At least two attempts in 1984 were similarly thwarted.

Doe proceeded with the scheduled October 1985 election, which international observers noted was a mockery of the process. A new constitution was passed naming Doe head of state, head of government, and commander-in-chief of the armed forces.

The current civil war began in December 1989 when Libyan-backed followers of Charles Taylor (a former Doe supporter) invaded Liberia from camps in the Ivory Coast. In 1990 the conflict quickly escalated, Doe opponents splitting into factions under the leadership of Charles Taylor and Prince Johnson. Johnson held Monrovia and its immediate environs while the countryside was controlled by Taylor. Doe was captured and killed, but Taylor and Johnson continued their struggle for personal power that led to the slaughter of many thousands of unarmed civilians.

Embarrassed by the carnage, members of the Economic Community of West African States, ECOWAS (Sierra Leone, Guinea, Nigeria, Gambia and Ghana) met to discuss how they might bring an end to the conflict. They hammered out an "ECOWAS Peace Plan" for an interim government to be succeeded by any elected government chosen by internationally-observed elections within twelve months. Soon after, ECOWAS sent troops into Liberia and took an increasingly active stance in the fighting. A loose alliance developed between the forces of Doe's remnant fighters, the Johnson rebels and ECOWAS forces. In mid-November 1990, the trio succeeded in getting Taylor to agree to a cease-fire, and installed Amos Sawyer, a former Liberian professor, as president of the interim government. Johnson surrendered to the military arm of ECOWAS.

Prospects for peace gradually improved. An ECOWAS mediation team attempted to settle disputes, but the plan stalled when Taylor announced he would talk to the mediation team only if Libyan troops were included in ECOWAS and he himself allowed to choose neutral ground for future negotiations. Taylor became increasingly unpredictable and a succession of attempts to bring about an end to the conflict fell into disarray.

The United States, involved in the original establishment of the republic, with many close ties to Liberia over the years and more recently as a Doe supporter, would seem to have a moral obligation to help end the conflict. In October 1990 a Sawyer delegation came to the U.S. to elicit international support for the peace process and for rebuilding the country. President Sawyer addressed the U. N. General Assembly and also met with Jimmy Carter. Much to its credit, The Carter Center sent in a team to monitor a national election. But by the end of 1992 the West African Peacekeeping Forces found themselves resisting embroilment in an escalating war, and Carter personnel had to be airlifted to safety.

By July 1993 an estimated 150,000 Liberians had been killed and 750,000 refugees had fled the country. Charles Taylor had reneged on some twenty agreements to a cease fire; but increasing ECOWAS military and economic pressures, and a week of negotiations sponsored by the United Nations and facilitated by the Carter Center, resulted in more promising talks on July 10. An accord dated July 25 was signed by Charles Taylor's National Patriotic Front, President Amos Sawyer's interim Government of National Unity, the United Liberation Movement for Democracy and the Armed Forces of Liberia.

The accord pledged to cease fire, disarm and disband under supervision of U.N. Security Council observers, to allow relief convoys to reach about 100,000 civilians cut off by the fighting in the northwest, and to work with the U.N. High Commissioner for Refugees for a speedy return of those who had taken flight.

Relief shipments in August established a significant lifeline to the north where hundreds of children were reported dying weekly from malnutrition and disease.

We have just learned that, at great risk, ways have been found to keep Ganta hospital and leprosy hospital open and functioning. By the time you read this report, we hope Liberia will be well on the way to recovery.

Elsie H. Landstrom
Conway, Massachusetts
1 November 1993

Elsie H. Landstrom
*Photo by Peter MacDonald,
Greenfield Recorder*

Chief surgeon at Wuhu General Hospital in China for more than two decades before enlarging medical services at the Ganta Mission in Liberia, Hyla S. Watters was a diminutive woman of formidable talent and great goodness who put her own comfort and safety far behind dedication to her work. Inspiring companion volumes, *Hya Doc, Surgeon in China Through War and Revolution, 1924-1949* and *Hyla Doc in Africa, 1950-1961* make thoughtful gifts.

Please send:

_____ copies of *Hya Doc, Surgeon in China Through War and Revolution* ($12.95 each)

_____ copies of *Hya Doc in Africa* ($10.50 each)

To (please use a separate sheet for additional names):

NAME: _____

ADDRESS:_____

CITY/STATE/ZIP:_____

PHONE: (   ) _____

Send this form or a facsimile, along with $2.00 shipping and handling for one book (add $1.00 for each additional book; Connecticut residents add 6% sales tax) to:

E. S. Allen, 520 Old Post Road, Tolland, CT 06084

Please allow 2-4 weeks for delivery.

Recent Titles from QED Press

Fiction

The Long Reach by Susan Davis
An "eternal, expansive and heady love story."
$12.95   204 pages (paper)   ISBN: 0-936609-27-3

Tales From The Mountain by Miguel Torga (Ivana Carlsen, trans.)
The first American translation of fiction by Portugal's Nobel Prize nominee.
$12.99   160 pages (paper)   ISBN: 0-936609-23-0
$21.99   160 pages (case)   ISBN: 0-936609-24-9

Coz by Mary Pjerrou
A young midwife is thrust into an elemental, cosmic battle.
$10.95   224 pages (paper)   ISBN: 0-933216-70-X

Art

Paris Connections: African American Artists in Paris (Belvie Rooks, Asake Bomani, eds.)
American Book Award prize winner. Bilingual (French/English) essays with full-color reproductions, biographies, bibliography, index.
$30.00   128 pages (paper)   ISBN: 0-936609-25-7

Paris Connections: African and Caribbean Artists in Paris (B. Rooks and A. Bomani, eds.)
Bilingual (French/English) essays on African and Caribbean artists in Paris.
$14.95   64 pages (paper)   ISBN: 0-936609-26-5

Psychology/Counseling

Listening with Different Ears, Counseling People Over 60 by James Warnick
A practical guide for dealing with the problems confronting an aging population.
$19.50   224 pages (paper)   ISBN: 0-936609-28-1
$24.95   224 pages (case)   ISBN: 0-936609-31-1

Living Well With Chronic Illness by Gayle Heiss
Coping with the complex challenges of day-to-day living with a chronic illness.
$2.00   16 pages (paper)   ISBN: 0-936609-10-9

The Collected Works Of Lydia Sicher: An Adlerian Perspective (Adele K. Davison, ed.)
Lydia Sicher, M.D., Ph.D., provides insights into the psychotherapeutic process.
$24.95   572 pages (paper)   ISBN: 0-936609-22-2

Biography

Hyla Doc: Surgeon in China Through War and Revolution (Elsie Landstrom, ed.)
A young doctor treats the diseased and wounded in war torn China.
$12.95   310 pages (paper)   ISBN: 0-936609-19-2

Men And Birds In South America: 1492 - 1900 by R. Stowell Rounds
Brief biographies of European ornithologists in South America.
$14.95   204 pages (paper)   ISBN: 0-936609-16-8

Business

Take This Job and Sell It! The Recruiter's Handbook by Richard Mackie
Earn $100,000 a year at home placing professionals with mid-sized companies.
$24.95   160 pages (paper)   ISBN: 0-936609-30-3
$34.95   160 pages (case)   ISBN: 0-936609-29-X

Available from your local bookstore or from QED Press
155 Cypress Street, Fort Bragg, CA 95437 (707) 964-9520.